Ann Miller Kontz & Other Husband Killers

Belinda Maddox

Published by Trellis Publishing, 2021.

While every precaution has been taken in the preparation of this book, the publisher assumes no responsibility for errors or omissions, or for damages resulting from the use of the information contained herein.

ANN MILLER KONTZ & OTHER HUSBAND KILLERS

First edition. July 12, 2021.

ISBN: 979-8224116447

Written by Belinda Maddox.

ANN MILLER KONTZ & OTHER HUSBAND KILLERS

BELINDA MADDOX

With her blonde and slightly tangled bob hairstyle and tense nervous smile, Ann Miller Kontz sat waiting anxiously for the Judge to ask her the inevitable question she was dreading.

She stood before her panel of deciders – attorneys, court appointed scribes and jury members; her petite frame barely noticeable in amongst the bustling lawyers in their striped suits and wads of paper.

If they were expecting a circus, she was not going to give it to them. She was not going to share anything of what put her in that seat and in that courtroom that day.

Its November 2005, the weather is cold outside but the heat in the courtroom is palpable.

"I would like to make a statement to the court on behalf of my client."

It's not sure when Ann Miller Kontz decided to plead guilty, or even if it was part of a larger more elaborate plan to fool those around her, but the relief in the families of the victim could be seen etched on their faces when the statement was made. Guilty for second degree murder; Guilty in the first degree on conspiracy to commit murder. In other words, she had decided that despite being the one to end her husband's life, she was not entirely responsible, and, only knowledgeable in the fact that death could, and would, inevitably occur with the actions she had taken.

Before the court sat a 35-year-old woman, but years before and as Ann Brier, she was the ideal American sweetheart. Ann was born to be successful. Surrounded by a well-structured, loving and successful family, Ann was born in 1970; the first of three siblings. With doting parents, a beautiful home in a quiet and respectable neighbourhood and, an easy and comfortable life most of us would envy, it seemed that Ann had been handed to keys to a great and exciting life ahead.

Her family were well educated and financially secure. From a strong middle-class background, Ann not only excelled in her school in terms of academics, but held every characteristic of a stunning and immensely popular student. Sporty, pretty and fun to be around, Ann seemed to have it all.

The town in which she grew up in, Spring Grove, Pennsylvania, was very much like her future – idealistic and full of promise.

Ann Brier left her school in Pennsylvania with exceptionally good grades and a strong sporting resume in tow. With her immense knack for chemistry and math, it was almost preordained that she would take her career further and in those fields in particular. Picking up her studies and fascination with all things chemical, Ann took on a tough degree in Chemistry at Purdue University, and continued on her well thought out future that encompassed a clear vision of a successful and, indeed wealthy lifestyle for herself.

It was at Purdue University that Ann first met and fell head over heels for a young and ambitious Eric Miller. Eric was not only handsome, but studying within the same field as Ann – it was a picture-perfect relationship with the same trappings as that of a Hollywood super couple. Known fondly as the local Ken and Barbie, the couple soon became inseparable.

Eric himself came from a reasonably wealthy middle class and tight knit family and was destined for a great and successfully financial future. He too had loving parents who had set him up toward a strong career and of course, enjoyed his sport and was athletically fit.

The two were inextricably linked and madly in love as most young and vivacious couples are. Studying hard, both of them excelled in their various fields and their relationship continued to blossom. It was not long before the two made serious plans for their perfect and future lives together.

After completing their degrees and graduating in 1992, Eric proposed to his sweetheart on Valentine's day, cementing what would seem to be the ideal love and life together. For Ann, and as she gleefully blurted to her friend, she was marrying the man of her dreams.

Little did Eric know that the greed simmering deep within Ann would be his ultimate and tragic downfall - after all they were in love; they were a beautiful couple; they were both ambitious and set on a great career ahead.

Lust and greed are the most powerful emotions that drive one to do and say the craziest things – drive you to take the life of another without the slightest hesitation.

But before the cold and calculated tragedy was to unfold, Eric and Ann were still so very much in love and after marrying in 1993, the couple moved to Raleigh, a beautiful up and coming suburb full of potential and beauty.

Before long Eric and Ann were well and truly settled and by 1998, Eric had opted to rather accept a federal grant to study and conduct research in paediatric Aids. An honourable role to take on and for such a worthy cause, however not exactly a matching salary or income to the plans the two of them had together. This may not have suited Ann as she was very much into maintaining a certain lifestyle and standard. Ann was a Madonna 'Material Girl', set on the finer things in life and all the appearance that money could buy.

But with a husband who was not dropping down on his standards, Ann decided to pack in the PhD that she was pursuing and sought a high paying job to keep her life on track. Taking on a sought-after position as a Chemist and Researcher for an international firm, Glaxo Smith Kline, Ann began to roll in the money she craved and the material possessions that came along with such a high paying salary.

Very much into her own appearance, Ann made sure her hard earned salary was spent on her looks – opting for a boob job and several forms of plastic surgery. Her trips to the spa and her constant splashing out on hair, make-up and nails, meant she always looked her best. In fact, her drive to be the perfect Barbie girl, ensured she remained popular amongst her male colleagues.

It was this fatal attraction that put Derril Willard, her colleague firm and squarely into the picture. Derril worked at Glaso Smith Kline as a drug maker and the two quickly became friendly. Derril was himself happily married at the time with a young daughter and, by 2000 Ann had given birth to her beautiful daughter, Claire.

It seemed that the world was their oyster, but like the dark depths of a troubled ocean, the relationship between Ann and Eric would blacken to the point of callous murder.

In her new role at Glaxo Smith Kline, as a prominent researcher, Ann was of course privy to and had easy access to all sorts of chemicals – good and bad. She was a clever individual who had excelled in Chemistry and knew her way around extracting and administering the right doses to ensure the right outcome. Her job paid well and she was held in high regard amongst her colleagues and peer. A few years had ticked by for Ann in her new and exciting role and by 2000, Ann was well on her way to cementing a secure and well-paying future. That same year, Ann began socializing more prominently with her work colleagues, taking Eric along to meet her friends and, her new and closer friend, Derril Willard. Despite being pregnant at the time, Ann managed to happily juggle her demanding job, family life and pregnancy with reasonable ease.

On one particular evening that year, Ann took Eric along to a get-together with her GSK colleagues for a night of bowling and fun. Of course, Derril Willard was amongst the group of friends. Eric picked up his newly ordered bottle of beer and happily smiled at the jokes and conversations filling the bowling hall. As he took a sip of his beer, he frowned, slightly hesitated and then remarked how the beer seemed to be slightly off. But none the wiser, Eric continued to drink his beer and tried to enjoy the evening's proceedings. Food, fun and alcohol were flowing and Ann was most certainly in her element. But a short while after he had finished his beer, a wave of nauseating pain flushed through his body and he slumped in agony complaining of sever stomach ache. Everyone thought it must have been some food poisoning, including Eric, but as the even ticked by, Eric felt his world collapse around him and Ann quickly and anxiously took him off to hospital.

Eric spent several days recovering from what could only be described as a serious case of food poisoning – or so everyone thought, even the medical staff at the hospital. Doctors were baffled on the illness that had suddenly best Eric. After all, Eric was a strapping young 30-year-old who had apparently and indeed, quite rapidly succumbed to some strange kind of poisoning while out and about with his wife and friends. But nonetheless and, after several days of rest and recuperation, Eric was discharged with his medicine and none the wiser as to what was to come just a few weeks later – his life would end - violently. His wife guilty of poisoning him.

A week passed and Eric, although still rather numb for his bad bout of supposed food poisoning, seemed to be getting better – albeit slightly. Things picked up and the routine of playing house soon ensued with Ann making her weak husband some hearty meals. Eric's life was about to drastically change when he again, fell violently ill after eating dinner with his wife at home. Loyal, pretty and petite Ann, quickly rushed him to hospital again. This time however, Eric was in a much worse state than before, thrashing and convulsing on the table. Doctors immediately took various blood tests and did their best to stabilize him.

Frail and close to death, Eric lay half comatose and hooked up to an IV bag – his life line of medication that was there to try and fight this unknown and vicious illness that had beset him. Ann sat quietly by his side, soothingly stroking his arm and exhibiting all the traits of a young and distraught wife in love. The hustle and bustle of busy emergency life continued down the corridors of the hospital. But, in the silence of his hospital room, Ann reached down into her handbag, carefully feeling around for something. Her nimble fingers finding the article her eyes and mind were searching for, wrapped carefully around the object and raised it from the darkness of her bag. Ann had taken out a syringe that was filled with an unknown substance. Unknown to us, but to Ann, she knew just how deadly the substance was that was murkily floating around inside that syringe. Carefully and methodically like a trained nurse, Ann Miller Kontz injected the contents into Eric's IV bag and then patiently sat waiting; staring ahead with cold callous eyes.

Within a few short minutes, Eric's fate was sealed. By the cold morning of December 2nd, 2000, Eric had succumbed to the poisons that ravaged his body. He was thirty years old. His only crime was loving his wife.

Doctors who had frantically tried to save Eric and had sent off numerous blood tests, were shocked to eventually discover the deadly illness that had befallen this young fit man. They had discovered the arsenic in his body, but unfortunately they had discovered it too late to save a man who would never have realized that the woman of his dreams, was the one who was there to murder him.

Police were called and an investigation was launched. After all, someone lying dead on a slab had been pumped full of arsenic – not just once, but over several months according to the toxicology reports.

It could only be someone close to him and who had exclusive uninhibited access that could pull off such a brutal murder. But evidence is always needed to prove what everyone suspects.

Police Investigator, Chris Morgan, with his unusual and somewhat eccentric Fedora hat-wearing appearance, set about seeking the evidence he needed to build a case.

Despite search warrants on the home of Ann and Eric; witness statements and here say, police made very little progress. No direct proof or data could link Ann to her husband's sickening demise. As Ann dispassionately hid away from the world, funeral plans were made and Eric laid to rest.

Five gruelling years came and went, but no truth could release the pain of Eric's family who were crying out for justice to be served.

The cold widow of Raleigh eventually took her young daughter and moved to her sister in ...

But the eccentric Morgan would not let the case go – even with retirement looming just a few months away, the inspector extended his time on the case in order to seek out the truth and bring Ann to justice. He knew she had poisoned her husband. He knew she had the means and the access to the fatal poison. But did she have motive? This was a young, successful and beautiful woman who had everything going for her. A new mother of young daughter, Claire just a few months earlier and with what seemed, no obvious hiccups in life. A clean slate – but an obscure and dark obsession for money and men.

Motive came in the form of the unsuspecting Derril Willard.

At the time of Eric's death, Derril had made contact with his own private attorney named Rick Gammon. Under attorney client privilege, Derril affirmed the conversations and relationship he had with Ann Miller and, specifically a conversation between the pair regarding Ann's actions on one of the evenings in the hospital room where Eric lay fighting for his life.

Before Morgan could press Derril to come clean on his role in the death of Eric, Derril took a gun and shot himself in the garage of his own home; leaving a sad and wretched suicide note. Derril's unsuspecting wife found his limp body and the letter pouring out his apology to her and his young daughter. He claimed his innocence in the wrongful death of Eric, but confessed that he would be blamed in some way. He maintained that he was only responsible for taking his own life – his own. He had paid the ultimate price of knowing Ann – his wife and daughter had paid a higher price.

Derril's suicide came just a month after Eric. At the time of Eric Miller's untimely death, Morgan had questioned Derril on his relationship with Ann during an issued warrant to search his premises.

Morgan recalled how Derril had sat gloomily while his house was torn apart by police in the hunt for evidence and, let slip that he had been indeed done over by Ann.

More surreal than the events surrounding Derril's suicide, is that Ann, just a few days after the suicide of her supposed lover, took off with her daughter and moved in with her sister in Wilmington, North Carolina.

Attorney Gammon continued to feel the mounting pressure from the Raleigh police force – but to maintain his integrity as a lawyer, Gammon refused to disclose the nature and content of any conversation he had written or documented with Derril.

For Derril's wife, Evette, she was left distraught and confused – her husband's suicide note and, of course the mere fact that he had taken on the advice of a private lawyer specifically regarding the murder of Eric, meant he must have in some way, been involved. Her young daughter and her own life, had become horribly entangled in a case that would continue to drag on for several long and painful years.

Morgan and the Raleigh police would not give up even when Ann had moved out of town leaving destruction and pain in her wake. Eric's father, Verus Miller, continued to plead with authorities to find the person responsible for his son's death. His son, who had a bright future; a beautiful daughter and a loving mother, father and sister who would not give up on him.

Ann quietly continued her life, eventually marrying a Christian Rock Musician and taking on his surname as an extension to hers – now Ann Miller Kontz, she waited inevitably for the law to catch up with her.

By late 2005, almost five years to the day of Eric's murder, police eventually found a break in the case. Through a complicated and lengthy process, Raleigh Police eventually managed to successfully implement an indictment against Gammon, the late Derril Willard's lawyer, forcing him to disclose the contents of the conversations he had with Derril prior to his suicide.

Forced to reveal the details, Gammon turned over his notes to police and Inspector Morgan who quickly set about unravelling the truth behind Eric's demise. Willard had conveyed the conversation he and Ann had just after Eric's death. He had told Gammon that Ann had confessed to injecting something into the IV bag at the hospital and that she had intentionally taken Eric's life.

The end for Ann was near. A young 35-year-old woman now stood on trial for the murder of her husband. She had poisoned him with arsenic. But, before the case could fully proceed to court, Ann Miller Kontz, to the surprise of all, admitted to conspiring with her lover, the late Derril Willard, to poison Eric.

Investigator and now retired police member, Chris Morgan, who had pushed for justice for a number of years, could now breathe a sigh of relief. He could bring peace to Verus Miller, Eric's distraught father. He could now lay to rest, Eric whose life had been so abruptly and cruelly ended.

In that perfect life and idealistic picture of a beautiful ambitious couple, hid a deeper more sinister motive. Ann Miller Kontz, who was successful; liked by many; popular; enjoyed a stable and good upbringing; worked hard at school and made top grades; met the man of her dreams – a handsome, articulate and loving individual who was going places; achieved a wonderful degree and took on a high paying role in a well-known reputable organization – all of that was not enough for her. She wanted more – what she was trying to find, is beyond most of our understanding.

According to Investigator, Chris Maddox, the motive was a simple one. Ann Miller Kontz was not satisfied with the life she was living. It did not match the lifestyle she had envisaged for herself those few years ago when she sat dreaming of her future as a young and beautiful teen. Despite a handsome husband and new-born and, a great paying job, the obstacle that was preventing her from reaching her pinnacle, was Eric. Eric needed to be removed so that she could build the life she wanted and, more importantly, believed she deserved. If she could remove Eric Miller from her life, she could have it all. She could have a new man – a man that would keep her greed fulfilled.

Now at just thirty-five years of age she was going to prison for life. Ann Miller Kontz was sentenced in November 2005 to between 25 and 32 years in prison for the murder of her husband, Eric. Clare, the innocent daughter was only six years old at the time her mother was taken away. She may not ever truly remember her father, except some brief moments and some photos of her smiling dad holding her close. The earliest that Ann Miller Kontz will be eligible for parole will be in 2029. She is now 48 and it is unlikely she will see her freedom or her daughter Clare, until she is the ripe old age of 70. That is if Clare would even want to see her. How do you come to terms with knowing that your parent – your mother – is a murderer? And not only a murderer of a stranger, but the convicted killer of your own flesh and blood. How far would Ann Miller Kontz have gone to, to achieve the lifestyle she wanted. If she had the cruel courage to take her husband's life, would she, could she have eventually found herself slowly poisoning her own daughter to remove yet another obstacle in her life?

Ann Miller Kontz is now thankfully and safely behind bars in Goldsboro Prison Facility in North Carolina – safely away from her daughter with whom she has no contact.

There is one more worrying piece of this obscure puzzle. Even though Ann handed herself into Police; even though she had now admitted to second degree murder and conspiracy to commit murder; we will never truly understand the role that Derril had played.

He had taken his life; blowing his brains out just a few months after Eric was so cold-heartedly murdered; imploring his wife and family to believe his final words that he was not involved. But why go to a lawyer and why would a murderer confess her actions to him if he was of no consequence to Eric Millar's death?

Faced with the reality of his own role; possibly his own words and actions that may have driven Ann to take that final step of injecting the lethal dose into Eric's IV bag. Eric's journey to death had begun just 5 months earlier – around the same time his young beautiful daughter was born.

How long had Ann been unhappy – or was she even unhappy? At what point did the planning begin – to take her husband's life in the most painful way she knew how – arsenic poisoning. Over months she sat there watching him eat his dinner, drinking his wine, smiling at her across the table and making small talk with the woman he loved and who he thought, loved him. Their first child on the way – no doubt she would have been a few months pregnant already before she had begun to spike his food with almost untraceable small doses of poison. It would have seemed the most impossible thought to him that his wife, of just a few years, was so bitterly calculating and evil.

How serious was the relationship between Derril and Ann? How long had they built up their relationship to the point that it had become so serious as to consider murder. Do we even know if the birth of Claire had been the beginning of the end for Eric, or, indeed even if Eric is the biological father of Clare?

Yes, Ann had moved on after Eric's death and Derril's death. Almost definitely more quickly than any of us would feel comfortable with. Her sudden departure of that quaint town epitomized her emotionless response to the impact she could have on other's lives. Narcassitic in her approach, Ann Miller Kontz, moved on physically and emotionally so quickly that she was soon married for two years to a Christian musician, living an entirely different life before her arrest. She had turned to God she claims – and that is the reason she turned herself in. But the truth is, she only turned herself in after she was formally indicted in September 2004. The truth had caught up with her and there was no place to run to now. Evidence had been found – and found in the haunting memories of a dead lover.

One murder can ruin so many lives and permeate so many facets of the towns and communities it touches. Ann's calculated and heartless act in taking Eric's young life, not only ruined her own future, but stripped her young daughter of a normal upbringing; brought her own parents down into despair and devastated the entire Miller family in one fail swoop.

Despite the many gaps and the speed at which things turned sour in the relationship between Eric and Ann, the only person alive who knows the full extent of the story, is the murderer. And, Ann Miller Kontz remains coldly quiet.

HUSBAND KILLER SHEILA DAVALLOO

NATHAN NIXON

Sheila Davalloo

Sheila Davalloo is truly one of the most demented individuals of the past twenty years. Several serious crimes are still being added to her gruesome resume. She portrayed the persona of a pleasant, happy person. She hid dark secrets, however, as to who she really was. The main victim was simply caught in a position that she could never escape from. To understand the vicious crime that Sheila Davalloo committed, it is important to understand the background of who she was. The totality of this murder is one that is still being uncovered. The lasting effects on an entire group of people has truly been catastrophic.

Sheila Davalloo was born on May 11, 1969 in Iran. She and her family immigrated to the United States in the mid-1970s. Like many other immigrants of the time, her family settled in New York in the town of Yorktown Heights. She obtained a great education while in the United States. She excelled in her classes and graduated near the top of her class. She was one of the most committed students in her school during her time there. Her family had really instilled a strong sense of pride in learning and continued education. She went on to go to college at SUNY Stony Brook on Long Island. This was a great location for her as it allowed her to stay close to home. Her family had a close bond and desired to have a strong relationship with Sheila. She went on to earn a degree in biochemistry in four years of schooling. This is an advanced degree and requires great dedication. This speaks to the mind of Sheila Davalloo and her ability to think logically and on a higher level than most.

Just after graduating college, she went on to start her life according to the "American Dream". She married her first husband, Farid Moussavi, in the year after her graduation. Farid was a close family friend that the Davalloo family had known for many years. He was a business man who had established a strong reputation in the area. Their marriage, however, would not last long. It is well understood that Sheila was never in love with Farid. This marriage went back to the culture of the Middle East of the time of family approved marriage. This was more of a marriage to appease the wants of her family. Her next step would lead her to cross paths with her gruesome reality.

Sheila Davalloo attended graduate program classes New York Medical School. She desired to apply her knowledge and move up to a bigger scale. It was at her graduate school class that she met a man named Paul Christos. Paul was an honest man. Sheila did not wear her wedding ring in most public places. Paul never had any idea that Sheila was married. After several months of friendly communication, the two started an affair on a grand scale. Sheila would frequently find excuses to come home later than normal from school. Paul was falling madly in love with Sheila, as she was him. Sheila knew that she could not divorce Farid, as it would be a disgrace to her family. After several months of sneaking around, Farid found out of Sheila's affair. He immediately filed for divorce and flushed her out of his life.

In 2000, Paul and Sheila married and moved into an upscale condominium. The location of the condo was 21 Foxwood Drive, Pleasantville, New York. The location of their residence would prove to be vital to the case.

Sheila seemed to be settled down in her new life. She was married to a man of her choosing, at her time. She had obtained a great job as a research scientist at Purdue Pharma in Stamford, Connecticut. This job was something that she had always wanted. She had always valued education and, to her family, this was the culmination of those efforts. However, something else would catch her attention at this new job.

Also working at Purdue Pharma was a man named Nelson Sessler. Sessler was a highly intelligent man. He was a lead scientist for the company and someone that had established a strong reputation of hard work, dedication, and integrity. When Sheila met Nelson Sessler, the two immediately hit it off. They were always working together and hanging out together on their breaks throughout the day. It was apparent to anyone that the two were flirting and very personal together. In a similar situation, Nelson Sessler had no idea that she was married.

Sheila Davalloo went to great lengths to protect her marriage and work from her affair. The lies she maintained and the stories she made her husband to believe were nothing short of strange and demented. Sheila became extremely enamored with Nelson. The pair had struck up a steamy affair that really had no limits. Sheila was desperate to establish a secondary life with Nelson Sessler. To do this, she convinced her husband Paul Christos to leave their house while still staying "happily" married. Davalloo told him that her schizophrenic brother would be staying over at their house. She named this brother Shahiem. Shahiem had no idea that she was living with anyone and would lose his sanity if he knew. At least, that is what Sheila told Paul. Paul didn't necessarily understand the odd request, but was happy to oblige to help his wife. Paul Christos packed up all of his belongings and moved in with his parents. This was odd to everyone around the situation.

Upon Paul leaving to his parent's house, Sheila Davalloo hid anything and everything that would give any indication that she was married. Shahiem obviously didn't exist. Shahiem was in all actuality Nelson Sessler. Sheila invited Sessler to stay over. Nelson was honestly a bit suspicious of the whole situation. Sheila convinced Nelson that she was divorced and happily single. While Nelson did not live with Sheila at this point, he spent many nights at Davalloo's home and they continued a steamy, one-sided affair.

Sheila was an educated woman who had progressed rapidly in her career. She understood human thinking at a high level, and understood that she had problem. At the beginning of 2002, she began to see a psychiatrist. She was still respectful of her marriage to a point that she didn't want to divorce Paul, however she admitted in September of 2002 that she always maintained a fantasy with Nelson. Her affair continued. Her communications with her psychiatrist would prove to be crucial after her crimes and would be used to find the true facts to her mindset in the case.

On Sunday, March 23, 2003, Sheila and Paul were spending a quiet afternoon relaxing at their home. Their marriage had been slowly pressing on, however their love life had almost screeched to an immediate halt. Sheila suggested that they play a game that she had learned at work. Sheila was becoming very flirtatious, so Paul was fully up to agree to the game. The pretext of the game, she described, was that he had to be handcuffed and blindfolded. Thinking this was going to turn into a romantic, kinky sex game, he readily agreed. Little did he know what was about to happen. Sheila lavishly blindfolded Paul and handcuffed his hands behind his back. Sheila was about to do the unthinkable.

Sheila Davalloo produced a 4 inch long paring knife from the kitchen. She violently stabbed her husband, Paul Christos, in the chest. The stabbing fully penetrated his chest, sinking the blade over 3 ½ inches into his chest cavity. Immediately, Paul panicked and begged her to stop. Sheila screamed out that it had been an accident. She was ever convincing and Paul was super naïve. He begged her to let him out of the handcuffs, however Sheila claimed that she lost the key to the handcuffs. Paul Christos lay there bleeding out, his life hanging by a thread and contingent on receiving medical attention.

Paul began to tell Sheila to call 911. Sheila left the room to call 911, and returned minutes later and told Paul that the line was busy. Paul was still handcuffed at this time. He had been stabbed in the heart, and was literally bleeding to death internally. Next, Sheila tried to get a doctor that was nearby to come to the house. She left the house for over ten minutes, but returned only to find Paul still alive. She told him that the doctor was closed. She the magically found the handcuff keys. She released Paul from the handcuffs and took the blindfold off of him. In her mind, she thought that he would be dead soon.

Sheila Davalloo loaded Paul into the back of her car. He was clinging to life, and seemed to be fading rapidly. She calmly and slowly drove to the hospital. Ironically enough, she didn't even go to the emergency room when she arrived at the hospital. Paul was begging her to hurry up. In Paul's mind, this was still an accident. He still believed that Sheila didn't mean to stab him with the knife. He would quickly learn the truth in a matter of minutes.

Upon arriving at the hospital, Sheila bypassed the emergency room entrance and instead parked the car at a secluded lot far towards the back of the hospital. She exited the front door of the car, and opened the back door. At approximately 5:30 P.M. Sheila stabbed her husband Paul Christos a third time, severely piercing his heart. This would be a near lethal wound. This time, however, there was a witness to the event. An onlooker from the Behavioral Health Center saw the confrontation taking place between Davalloo and Christos. The onlooker immediately called 911 to get help to the scene. Davalloo fled the scene and left Christos for dead in the back of her car. Davalloo was found by the authorities and quickly rushed into the emergency room. He was put to the top of the line and urgently taken into the operating room where he would undergo extensive open heart surgery.

The onlooker seeing the confrontation ultimately saved Paul Christos's life. Without the call, Sheila likely would have left him for dead in the back of that car and he would have been dead in minutes. Sheila also saved his life herself by taking him to the hospital. Hopeful that this would clear her name and prove it to be some sort of accident, she believed that he would not make it to the hospital. When he was still clinging to life upon their arrival there, she decided to stab him again to finish the job. Ultimately, the fact that he was so close to the hospital is the only way he managed to survive this brutal stabbing. Had this wound happened at their home, he likely wouldn't have even made it to the hospital alive.

In a further twist of irony in this already wildly bizarre case, Sheila Davalloo actually fled the scene AND CAME BACK! She fled the scene after stabbing Paul for the third time in her car. She came back to get Paul out of the hospital. She screamed at hospital personnel demanding they release him to her. Police were notified and rushed to catch her before she could escape. Unfortunately, she escaped out of the hospital. Police finally caught up with her. She was arrested by Mount Pleasant police. They took her to the primary jurisdiction, which was the Westchester Police Department. She was finally in custody. Paul was given a 50 percent chance to live through the recovery of the surgery. His body was in an extremely fragile state and his heart had been badly injured. While the surgery had successfully stopped the bleeding and fixed the apparent injuries, the trauma had taken quite a toll. Paul was left in intensive care to recover from his devastating attack. Police questioning would yield a strong sense of confusion and anger as they struggled to get any sort of truth from Sheila.

Police of the Westchester Police Department began their questioning of Sheila Davalloo that evening. She was questioned most literally all night. Police statements describe Sheila as being unwilling to vacate her story of it all being an accident. She initially explained that Paul's injuries were not even inflicted by her. Her story stated that his injuries were caused when he was working in New York City. This was an outlandish story obviously, however police investigated quickly to determine there was no truth to this. Nonetheless, police had enough evidence to hold her in jail with no bail set. This was crucial for the rest of the investigation.

Investigators needed to talk with Paul Christos to get his testimony. However, while he was recovering and looked as though he would survive the horrific incident, he was obviously in no condition to give credible information. Police needed his story, however they were forced to wait. Investigators looked to other sources to acquire more evidence and, perhaps, an explanation to this unbelievable act.

The police investigation team decided it would be a good idea to look at her cell phone records. Sheila had told investigators that she tried to call 911. She was adamant about this fact, being as how her story was based around a work incident that she tried to solve by taking Paul to the hospital. What police found was shocking. Police found out that she not only never called 911, she called someone by the name of "Nelson". This call took place at exactly 4:59 P.M. This means that she called "Nelson" during the stabbing. This was critical evidence to police.

Sheila Davalloo was vigorously questioned about "Nelson" and why this person would be called during the suspected accident timeframe. This was the only call she had made the entire time. Police found it suspicious that she not only lied about calling 911, but also that she only made a single phone call the entire time. Typically, when your husband has a catastrophic event such as this, or a workplace "accident" as she had suggested, then you would call some family to at least let them know what was going on. In such a dire situation, you would not load up the victim in the back of your car and park a quarter mile away from the emergency room entrance. While Sheila did not provide detail as to what was going on at this time or any sort of explanation, she did provide a solid piece of information. She declared to police that the man's last name was Sessler. This call was, in fact, to her lover Nelson Sessler. Police now had enough evidence to charge Sheila Davalloo. The following morning, she was officially charged with attempted murder in the first degree. Police now turned their attention to Nelson Sessler.

The following morning, March 26, 2003, Nelson Sessler was brought in for questioning in the case. Initially, he was believed to be a suspect. Police felt like he may have been an accomplice or "the help" within this heinous crime. Upon only a few minutes of questioning, police has informed Nelson Sessler that Davalloo was married to the victim, Paul Christos. Nelson Sessler genuinely had no idea. In all of the time they had been lovers, he had his suspicions, but none of them had been proven true. Sheila Davalloo had concealed this secret to him this entire time. Investigators asked him about the phone call that Sheila had made to him on the night of the stabbing. As grim as it is, he informed investigators that Sheila had asked him over for dinner that night around 8:30 P.M. This was a chilling declaration of the coldness of this crime. This also spoke to her true intentions with Paul; she wanted and expected to kill him. Nelson Sessler was cleared of any wrongdoing in the case. He was of no involvement in the crime, and Sheila herself agreed that he had not been at the house for weeks. This was the last piece of crucial evidence that police hoped would lead to the ultimate conviction of Sheila Davalloo for attempted murder of Paul Christos.

The final argument that the investigative team needed to make was a motive. To investigators, the motive became quite clear when looking back at the family history of Sheila as well as her previous marriage. To the Davalloo family, divorce was disgraceful. Sheila could not possibly divorce Paul and keep her spot in the family. She decided that if Paul had died, it would then make it respectable that she move on with her life. While this is a motive that could never be fully proven, police felt it offered the best explanation for the random attempted murder of her husband.

On February 4, 2004, Sheila Davalloo stood trial for attempted murder in the first degree for the stabbing of Paul Christos. The small courthouse in White Plains, New York was packed with people. This trial had drawn heavy regional attention and national attention as well.

Paul Christos, now recovered from his near fatal experience, explained to the courtroom that he had never before seen Sheila act so violently. He went into great detail of how she showed no urgency to help him with what he initially thought was a sick accident. He explained that she left him to die, handcuffed and blindfolded, and showed no worry for the entire situation. Davalloo pleaded not guilty in what appeared to be an impossible situation for her. The opening statement of the prosecution is one that littered newspapers around New York and regionally around the United States. They portrayed Sheila as a deceitful, extremely manipulative woman who had the intelligence to violently get what she wanted. They explained that she didn't want to shame her family with another divorce, so killing rather than walking away was her solution to save the embarrassment. The overall goal of the killing would be to successfully and peacefully remain with Nelson Sessler. To wrap up their statement, the prosecution team played the interrogation where Sheila lied repeatedly as to how Paul got his stab wounds. The opening statement, for all intents and purposes, tilted the case in the prosecution's favor beyond a doubt.

After a relatively short trial, the jury was set to deliberate and decide the fate of Sheila Davalloo. On February 18, 2004, jury deliberations began. The next morning, they had reached their decision. Before he read the verdict, Judge Thomas Dickerson told Sheila a chilling statement:

"You tried to kill your husband. You waited for him to die, and have lied over and over again. You are ultimately a dangerous threat to society."

Davalloo was then read her conviction. She was found guilty on attempted murder in the first degree as well as assault with a deadly weapon in the first degree.

"She is a very dangerous woman who thought she would get away with what she did," Alison Carpenter, a lead investigator on the case said. "I found her to be deceptive from the beginning. She is very calculating."

Davalloo's parents chose not to attend the trial. They had been shamed and felt completely embarrassed of their daughter's actions. Sheila did, ironically, maintain a close relationship with her in-laws. She was seen sitting with them during the breaks of the trial in hallways and meeting rooms. Ironically still, when court officials handcuffed her, she told them to give her purse to her mother-in-law.

The relationship between Sheila and Paul after the trial was one that would be impossible to predict. While Paul ultimately filed for divorce from Sheila, he maintained that he didn't want her to serve an extreme amount of jail time. He felt that she suffered from a severe mental illness and wanted her to get help for that. Even after being stabbed to the brink of death by Sheila, Paul still supported her and wanted her to get help. This speaks volumes to the man that Paul Christos was, as well as the deep spell that Sheila was able to cast on those that were close to her.

The judge did not provide a bail amount for Sheila. She was ordered to stay at the Westchester County Jail until her sentencing. Paul and others pleaded for her to not get a severe punishment. The minimum sentence in the state of New York for these charges was 5 years. On April 6, 2004, the judge sentenced Sheila Davalloo to the maximum sentence of 25 years. She was given no possibility of parole for the duration of the sentence. This was devastating, but most within the investigation and follow-up of the crime felt that it was a fitting punishment to such a cold blooded attempt at murder.

If this story ended there, it would be considered tragic. However, it does not. She was also involved in a successfully completed murder. The details of this one are chilling and really show that the judge got the sentencing right.

Sheila Davalloo was convicted in 2012 for the murder of Anna Lisa Raymundo. The murder happened on November 8, 2002. This was just 4 months before her attempted murder of husband Paul Christos.

Davalloo was dating Nelson Sessler at the same time that Sessler was dating Anna Lisa Raymundo. All three of them worked at Purdue Pharma together. When Sessler became involved with Raymundo, he ended his relationship with Davalloo. This enraged Sheila and left her seeking a solution. On November 8, 2002, at precisely 12:29 P.M. police received an anonymous phone call from a woman at a pay phone. The location of the phone was at a nearby restaurant on Shippan Avenue. This anonymous caller said that her neighbor was being viciously attacked by a large, light skinned male. Police went on to the condo to find the front door unlocked. When police opened the door, they were shocked to find the body of Anna Lisa Raymundo, lifeless and covered in blood, lying in the middle of the living room. The house was a mess. It was apparent to responders that there was a violent struggle that went on. Evidence to this included shattered glass all about, debris from all over the house, and blood spatters that were seemingly endless. High and low, it had all the look of a violent and heinous murder scene.

Autopsy records showed that Anna had been stabbed nearly 20 times. She had been severely beaten and had suffered a massive head trauma that likely knocked her unconscious. She also, mysteriously to police, had long hair in her hand. While this points to the struggle that police had suspected, it did not go with the initial figure that the anonymous caller had described.

In May of 2003, just 2 months after she was held for her attempted murder of Paul Christos, police announced that they were investigating a woman that Anna had worked with at Purdue. Since this announcement, evidence substantially mounted against one common person: Sheila Davalloo.

On November 6, 2007 Stamford police obtained a warrant to arrest Sheila Davalloo. Sheila was serving her sentence in New York for her attempted murder conviction. Police arrived at Bedford Hills Correctional Facility for Women where she was serving her 25 year sentence. They extradited her back to Connecticut to stand trial for the murder of Anna Lisa Raymundo on December 29, 2008.

Evidence against Sheila in this case was extensive. Most notably, security video shows her leaving Purdue Pharma shortly before 11 A.M. on the morning of the murder. DNA from bloodstains acquired at the scene matched both Sheila and Anna. The blood was found all over the house, but specifically a strong sample was found on two separate faucets around the house that show her efforts to clean the scene. The initial call that police received that day matches the voice of Sheila Davalloo. This was a chilling surprise in the case.

The extradition process for Sheila was not overly complicated. She agreed to be extradited to face trial for the murder of Anna Lisa Raymundo. She was initially tried on January 14, 2009 where she pleaded not guilty to the murder of Anna. After lengthy deliberation and a very odd trial, Sheila was ultimately found guilty of murdering Anna Lisa Raymundo and was sentenced to 50 years in a Connecticut State Prison.

Sheila still had to finish her initial sentence of 25 years, and then her 50 year sentence would start. She is set to be in jail until 2079. She will undoubtedly die in prison.

Sheila Davalloo has a story that is unique in that she naively believed that people would believe anything she said. This was held true by the lovers that she had in her life. The men that she was with all, undoubtedly, hung on to everything she said. She was able to carry on an affair for over 2 years without the other person even knowing that she was married. She convinced her husband, after stabbing him two times in the chest, that it was an accident. As crazy as this sounds, it is all fully true. The punishment that Sheila is currently serving is not near enough. Sheila Davalloo has proven to be one of the most vicious and naïve women of the past 20 years.

HUSBAND KILLER SHEENA EASTBURN

28

JAIMI WEST

Sheena Eastburn seemed to have the cards stacked against her from the start. She and Tim Eastburn were married young, when she had only just turned fifteen. The couple wed in 1990, although Tim was older, at twenty-one years of age. Talking many years later to the Joplin Globe, Alica Blevins- Sheena's mother- talked about how she should have guided her daughter's life differently, and put her on a different path.

"She was only 15 then. She was just a kid... Sheena was wild. I will admit that," she said. "For her and Tim, life was one big party. "She got herself in situations that got her into a lot of trouble. There were a lot of things that happened to her as a child that she never told me.

I just wish I could have done more for her when I had the chance. Maybe things would have turned out differently."

They were divorced a short two years later, which is often the case for couples married at such a young age.

While the divorce was described by friends as amicable, the couple maintained a sexual relationship over the years. Both were heavy drinkers, and took drugs together. In fact, whenever Sheena needed a fix, friends said, she would visit her ex-husband and provide sexual favours in return for drugs. The couple were still so close that they discussed remarriage.

Speaking about their relationship, Sheena would later say: "There were days when he loved me more than you could ever imagine and there were other days when we just fought. I was 15 years old when we got married. He was like a father and a husband to me. He was a wonderful man."

On or around November 1st, 1991, Sheena met Terry Banks for the first time, and the two immediately became close. When Banks learned of Sheena's continuing relationship with her ex-husband, however, he became "extremely possessive, jealous, and violent" according to court records. This was the catalyst for Tim's murder.

Tim Eastburn's murder

Tim was murdered using his own rifle, on November 19th 1992. He was shot in his own home in McDonald County, Missouri. The house is set a little back from the road, among the wooded hills common in McDonald County.

At the time of the murder, Sheena had only just turned seventeen, and her co-defendants were nineteen (Banks) and eighteen as well (Myers).

Two days previously, Sheena's co-defendants, Terry Banks and Matt Myers, had stolen Tim's gun- an AK-47- in a break-in along with a third man named Denashay, or 'D.J'. Johnson. They also took the chance to steal some of Tim's valuables, since stealing the gun on its own would have appeared suspicious.

The burglary took place only two weeks after Sheena had begun secretly dating her fellow co-defendant, Terry Banks. Tim and Sheena, Banks, Myers and Johnson were in fact all part of the same large circle of friends. In the time building up to the murder, the group had been drinking to excess and using drugs, a fact which probably gave the defendants the courage to do what they were about to do.

On the evening of November 19th, Sheena, Banks and Myers paid a visit to Tim at his home. It was only on that day that Sheena learned of the burglary at all; Myers and Banks had said they wanted to sell the gun- which would have fetched a good price- but Sheena convinced them not to, since it could be traced back to Tim through the serial number.

Sheena went in at first, alone, to talk with him. She asked him if he would like to come outside to take a ride on her motorbike, but he refused, saying that it was too late at night for him to want to go out.

At the time, Banks and Myers were hiding on the front porch. As Tim and Sheena continued talking, they walked through the house to the kitchen, where the pair kissed. It was only seconds later that Tim was shot with his own gun, through the window, by one of the pair outside. He quickly fell to the floor, and as he lay, Myers ran into the house to shoot him again to 'finish him off'. As he shot Tim for the second and final time, Sheena and Terry Banks ran from the house.

According to later interviews with Sheena, Tim's last words were "God forgive me for all my sins."

All three were arrested only days later, and each confessed separately to their role in Tim's murder. Each of their confessions were coherent, and none of the defendants contradicted the others with regards to their description of the day's events. However, Banks and Myers both claimed that Sheena had come up with the plot to murder Tim, a claim that she denied.

The Trial

Sheena was in prison for three years by the time she was finally put up for trial.

The facts of Tim Eastburn's murder were not challenged in court by either Terry Banks or Matt Myers. The only challenge made by Sheena was whether her actions were made after 'deliberation and cool reflection' or not- which is the metric by which murder in the first degree is judged under Missouri law. However, the defence also argued that Sheena did not necessarily understand her co-defendants' murderous intentions beforehand, a fact which also would have lessened the charge against her.

In testimony for her defence, Sheena claimed that she only learned of the burglary on the day of the murder itself. She believed that on the day that Tim died, the group of three were going to steal money and drugs from her ex-husband. She denied any knowledge of a plot to kill him. "I was supposed to go down there and get him out of the house, then we were going rob him for drugs and money."

They also planned to leave the gun at Tim's house after the robbery, rather than arouse suspicion by selling it. Sheena was quoted in interviews long after the trial, still standing by what she said. "The intent was to take back the gun that was stolen. They could track it down.

The timeline of the day's events suggested otherwise, however. Sheena's request for her ex-husband to follow her outside, and her bringing him to the kitchen with a window to the front of the house, suggested that she was trying to lead him to her death. At the very least, it was clear that it wasn't Sheena who fired the fatal shots from Tim's own gun. She claimed that Banks had shot him first in a fit of passion, after seeing the pair kiss. Myers had then delivered the final bullet.

After the shot was fired, Sheena said, "[w]e both dropped and when we dropped I crawled around to where he was, and I tried to stop the bleeding. There was nothing I could do." She was trying to paint a picture of innocence. She later talked about how she had tried to stop the bleeding with a towel and a sock that were lying nearby.

Over the course of the trial, extensive physical evidence was used in attempt to prove the group's guilt, almost sixty items in total. These included the rifle and the fragments of bullets found in Tim's body- which matched- and photo after photo of the crime scene.

D.J. Johnson also testified to the effect that the murder had been pre-meditated. He was actually a witness for the prosecution throughout the trial, as part of a plea bargain to help secure the verdicts of murder against the other three. As a result of his actions, he was given probation in connection to the charges of burglary against him, as he was part of the group that stole Tim's AK-47.

He testified that on the day of the murder itself, he overheard a three-way conversation between Myers, Banks and Sheena. In that conversation, Sheena discussed Tim with the others, claiming that he had raped her, and that she would love to see him dead. Banks, her then boyfriend, and Myers then both volunteered their services, according to Johnson. Sheena's attorneys made no attempt to discredit him, or disagree with any of his testimony.

The defence, however, argued that his testimony was unreliable due to its acquisition through a plea bargain. Johnson was offered freedom in exchange for his witness statements, and this perhaps did cast doubt on the truth of what he said. However, it was left for the jury to decide just what to make of his claims, and his statements formed a key part of the prosecution's case.

Prison Time

Whether the jury's decision would have been changed by any of this information must forever remain unknown. What they did decide, after a gruelling six hours, was that Sheena was guilty of first-degree murder.

Matt Myers was sentenced as the man who, according to the three confessions, had fired both of the fatal shots. Although he was only charged with second degree murder, among other offences related to Tim's murder (i.e. the burglary), he was sent to prison for a total of 67 years. Because of the murder being judged as of the second degree, he was eligible for parole throughout his sentence.

Terry Banks on the other hand, was sent to prison for life, on a charge of first degree murder. Sheena, too, was jailed with the same charge. The fact that Banks and Sheena were charged with first degree murder, whereas Myers (who fired one of the shots that killed Tim) wasn't, seems strange in hindsight. But Myers had made a plea bargain that saw him receive 'only' 67 years, but with the chance for parole in the future.

Indeed, Sheena's attorney filed a motion for post conviction relief in the immediate aftermath of the sentence, but this motion was denied.

"I really believed I was going to get second degree murder and I was accountable for that. I was okay with that," Sheena said in an interview, years later. She was visibly stunned when she learned of her sentence. "All I could hear was my mother in the courtroom... She was wailing," Sheena told KOAM TV. As part of the same news segment, Sheena's mother Alica Bleavins remembered the same scene: "I couldn't control it. When that's your child, and your only child, and your hands are tied..."

Terry Banks' story became more interesting in the year 2000, when he escaped from his maximum-security prison with the help of a guard. Lynnette Barnett smuggled Banks out in broad daylight, with the help of an old uniform and a fake ID. They were on the run for six weeks before they were caught. She was jailed for five years, with the help of video evidence and correspondence between her and Banks. She was, however, paroled within a year of her sentence.

Banks had another 16 years added to his sentence, although since he was already in prison for life with no option of parole, it makes little difference.

At the time of the escape, Sheena's mother said: "They put her on lock-down. They put her in the hole. They were going to leave her there until he was captured. The FBI, well, they were all over Sheena. She was the one who told them his dad was in Texas."

Signs of hope for Sheena?

There were several facts and allegations which weren't raised at trial, that in hindsight, should have been. Sheena's attorneys spoke publicly about how the outcome may have been completely different had they brought them up.

For one, IQ tests performed by Sheena in the buildup to the trial suggested that she would be incapable of organising the events as described by the prosecution.

There were also allegations that she had been raped by a McDonald County Jail when awaiting trial, and even taken to an abortion clinic. A guard who had been working there, Terrie Zornes, had been accused by Sheena of manipulating and raping her several times over the course of her time there. He had been 31, whereas she was still a minor.

Sheena claimed that he had taken her twice to the property room in 1994, and attacked her there. He was the only guard on duty at the time. According to interviews, Sheena had told her mother: "I told my mother that the officer had taken me to a property closet and had sex with me. She flipped out at that point. They locked me down in my cell. Cut off my phone. I wasn't allowed to talk to anybody. They cut off my visitors."

Multiple reviews of the surveillance tape from the nights that Sheena alleged she had been raped gave suspicious results. While nothing of note happened, at one point in the recordings the clock would jump forward. "The hands on the clock jumped forward. A clock doesn't do that," The Sheriff of McDonald County Jail later said.

The Sherriff had nonetheless defended Zornes, claiming that the sex was "consensual". Altogether, it seemed as if both the guard and the Sheriff felt that there was something to hide.

Sheena responded with revealing comments about her past. "They kept trying to tell me it was consensual. They said: 'You know you wanted it. You know you miss it.' It was not like I fought it because there was no way I could have stopped him. I have experienced sexual abuse all of my life. I have been raped before in a violent way. After you have been in that situation, you just learn it's easier to let it go and not fight."

Moreover, in the years since the case was closed, Myers recanted on his testimony at the trial that Sheena had been the mastermind of the operation. Kent Gipson, Sheena's long time attorney, had even attained an affidavit to that effect- and that he had acquired the same from Johnson, too. This would mean that in conjunction with their defence stemming from the low IQ test score, it would be possible to argue that Sheena could not have possibly wanted Tim to be killed that day.

These facts all gave Sheena hope that she could appeal her sentence, and perhaps, win. Even if she were only able to replace her sentence with one for second degree murder, she would at least be eligible for parole in the end.

Supreme Court challenge

In interviews after her sentencing, Sheena said: "I still thought that I might get out of prison someday... I didn't realize that life without parole actually meant life without parole." She continued to maintain her innocence, saying that she had never planned a murder that day, only a robbery.

In 2012, a case went through the Alabama Supreme Court which found that the sentence of life without parole was actually unconstitutional when handed down to a minor. The case came from Alabama, but because it had been decided by the Supreme Court, cases could now be challenged nationwide. Missouri, at the time, had 84 cases of juveniles jailed for life without parole and each one of them could now seek to have their sentences reduced.

Suddenly, it seemed that Sheena might have found a way out. Once more, Sheena contacted her attorney, and they began to prepare her case for appeal. Talking to KOAM TV, her attorney Kent Gipson said "I think if you look across the spectrum of persons convicted of first degree murder, I'd say her level of culpability is among the lowest I've ever seen."

Sheena's attorney believed that she had a great chance to finally be considered for parole; and both clearly believed that she deserved the chance. "I think inevitably she will be given a parolable sentence and will be given a chance to get out of prison," Gipson said at the time. Speaking about the progress she had made while in prison, he said "She's obviously not the same person she was when she was 17 years old, I don't think any of us are... She is probably the most ideal candidate for parole any of them [prison staff] have ever seen.""

Miles Parks, a retired investigator who had worked on the case, disagreed. "Sheena Eastburn was old enough to get a driver's license, old enough to get married, old enough to know the difference between right and wrong," Parks said. "What do you think is the appropriate punishment?"

In an interview before her appeal with KOAM TV, she talked about the possibility that she might be released. "I came to that realization a long time ago, and I gave it to God, and I got peace," she had said. She still maintained that she had no role in Tim's murder, saying that "[t]here was no reason for Tim to die... None."

With her interviewer, she discussed what she missed about the outside world: "...going down to the refrigerator in the middle of the night and being able to get what you want. Walking barefoot on grass somewhere that it doesn't say 'out of bounds'. Going outside after dark. Just taking time to experience free, fresh air... I know it smells different on the other side."

Sheena wished that she could somehow find release. But she still refused to get her hopes up, stating that "You never count on anything completely until it happens because you can't let yourself get your hopes too high and then be devastated all the time. It's just a hard way to live." Over her time in prison, she had clearly lived with a hope that one day she would be set free, but had only been disappointed.

The Post-Conviction Hearing

Close friends and relatives of Tim's did not want the case re-opened. Speaking in an interview, Bobby Eastburn said, "We have been keeping track of it. We don't like what is going on. She worked hard to get in there and we don't want her out of prison. "My brother won't get a second chance. She's apparently trying to get a second chance. They say she was suffering from PTSD because of her childhood and that she was not very smart. She manipulated the situation to kill Tim. She was the mastermind behind it. She was intelligent enough to set the whole situation up."

On April 30th of 2013, three cases of minors jailed for life were put before the Missouri Supreme Court- one of them being Sheena's. Her attorney argued that the original motion that had been filed way back in 1992, for post conviction relief, should not have been denied. They argued that the judge should have then realised that such a sentence was unconstitutional.

The state argued that they did not then have the authority to challenge the constitutionality of the sentence, and so they were correct to not have allowed the defendant's motion for relief. After both sides had been presented, the court took recess so that the judges could decide on their fate.

"I am definitely guilty of second-degree murder," Sheena said in an interview around the time of her appeal.

But whether or not her appeals would be successful, she felt all along that she could never be free. "For somebody with a case like this, the prison is not really the prison. It's always going to be inside. You will always be in prison. It does not matter whether you are free or locked up, I think you will always have that inside."

But on Tuesday 25th July, that year, the Missouri Supreme Court returned the unanimous verdict that her appeal did not stand. Based on the facts of the case, they still argued that it was necessary for Sheena to be imprisoned for life.

Sheena's final hearing

It turned out that Sheena would eventually win her appeal after all.

In 2015, Sheena appealed again, under the same Supreme Court ruling as before. In her hearing of October that year, she sought the sentence of second degree murder through a plea agreement with the prosecutor. To do so, Eastburn had to waive any and all post-conviction and appeal rights- which she did.

The hearing was only 25 minutes long in total this time around. Lou Kelling, a former sheriff and supporter of Eastburn's release on parole, said at the appeal, "This is what she should have been charged with to begin with. She was an accessory to the crime. She served 10 years more time than she should have served. That on top of the fact that she was mistreated while in custody."

The defence had indeed used the same arguments as in the prior appeal, including the evidence of Sheena's IQ test, and allegations of rape and forced abortion. This time, the court decided to vacate the prior judgement. Since she had been in prison for more than 23 years, the agreement made her immediately eligible for a parole hearing.

Parole at last

Sheena Eastburn is now set to be released from prison in November, 2017. She has been judged to have served her time for second degree murder, and is getting ready for life on the outside for the first time in her life as an adult.

In a telephone interview with the Joplin Globe after it became common knowledge that she was set to be released, Eastburn said: "I now know when I will be able to move on with my life. I am grateful for a chance at parole."

In the same interview, she described how she was planning to write to the parole board and the governor in the hope that she could demonstrate just how much she had changed during her time locked away from society. "I want to show that I can be successful outside of the prison," she said. "I am very sorry for the things that happened. I have changed my life and will make better choices."

In another interview, she described her plans for the outside world. "I would go to school to become a certified personal trainer. I would love to minister to juveniles and help them know that the choices we do make have a consequence. I really do want to help people. I know that sounds crazy. But I want to help and let them know there are other choices out there no matter what your life is like because I had a bad life and childhood, but I still had choices. I did not realize that then."

And it did indeed seem that she had made genuine effort to turn her life around. In a separate interview, Sheena's mother claimed that her daughter had made every effort she possibly could from within the prison system. "Sheena has completed all of the classes that they offer at the prison. She has taken everything ... She'll sit there and the taxpayers will pay $80,000 a year to feed and house her. If she had been let out, she'd have a job and feed herself. This is something I don't understand. But we are still grateful to have a release date."

"We have waited a long time for this day to come, but we don't know when she will be released. We don't have an out day yet," Blevins said. "It could be just a matter of some paperwork. No one can really say right now."

During her time in prison, Sheena had begun full time work as an obedience trainer for rescue dogs. On top of this full time job, she had also become a qualified aerobics instructor, and found occasional work in prison helping disabled inmates. On occasion, she even led victim counselling sessions. She had spent her time as wisely as she could, and it had given her inspiration for her future release.

Before her first appeal on the unconstitutional nature of her sentence, her attorney had said "Maturity and education, things like that, should be taken into account and that's all we're really asking, that she be given the opportunity to prove to the parole board and other people that she deserves a second chance."

By the end of this year, she will be getting that chance.

HUSBAND KILLER DONNA YAKLICH

41

JESSI DIXON

Old-fashioned police work

In December 1985, a narcotics detective was shot and killed in the driveway of his farm in Pueblo, Colorado, where he lived with his five children and his wife, Donna Yaklich. Initially, authorities suspected Dennis' death was linked to his work in law enforcement, but a tip led them to two teenage shooters – and eventually, back to Dennis' wife, Donna.

However, attorneys for Donna Yaklich argued that Dennis had been beating his wife. The murder, they claimed, was a battered woman's desperate attempt to escape a lifetime of abuse – or potentially becoming a murder victim herself, like Dennis' first wife, who is thought to have died of a diet drug overdose in 1977.

Yaklich was finally acquitted of first-degree murder after a mistrial and a second trial that has been described as "grueling," but was convicted on the charge of conspiracy for hiring gunmen to kill her husband. Her sentence was forty years in prison, but was released to a halfway house in 2005, after serving close to eighteen years.

The young men Yaklich had hired to carry out the murder were also arrested and sentenced. Charles Greenwell, who was only 16 when the crime was committed, received a sentence of twenty years while his brother Eddie, who had been 25, received thirty years.

However, while Yaklich's claims of abuse weren't enough to get her off on the premise of self-defence, they did encourage authorities to reopen their investigation into the death of Barbara Yaklich. According to a cold case team, the investigation was "incomplete."

"This case needed some good, old-fashioned police work," said team lead Steve Johnson, with the Colorado Bureau of Investigation. "In my opinion, I have seen better documented traffic accidents."

Discrepancies were found in the autopsy report, which originally claimed Barbara had fainted from taking diet pills. When her body-builder husband, Dennis, tried "energetically" to resuscitate her, she suffered bleeding in her abdomen. However, administering CPR is not an appropriate reaction to fainting – and as a police officer trained in CPR, Dennis would have known this.

Still, there was apparently no examination of the potential crime scene, and when Dennis was asked to take a polygraph to support his defense, he refused.

Denver-area pathologist Michael Doberson determined that the conclusions in the report were "very unusual" – the internal damage Barbara had suffered, he claimed, was more likely caused by a blow to the abdomen. Doberson included his findings in a letter to Johnson dated in 2005, stating that in his opinion, "the entire scenario is simply not credible." A second forensic pathologist concurred with Doberson's conclusions.

According to reports, Barbara's liver tore open and her abdomen was quickly filled with more than 2,000 millilitres of blood – nearly 40 per cent of her total blood volume, and more than twice as much as is typical in a victim of a fatal car accident.

Investigators are now considering her death as "suspicious," with the tear caused by a blunt force trauma consistent with "punches and knee drops to the upper abdomen," according to pathologist Stephen Cina. However, the autopsy report showed no other indications that would reveal a pattern of abuse – no recorded discoloration, bruising, or external signs of beatings.

While the investigation into Barbara's death is now complete, the case hasn't been closed. According to the coroner and the Pueblo County Sheriff, the public deserves answers to the questions that have been raised.

The family man

Donna Yaklich met Dennis and his children only a few months after Barbara's death. According to Yaklich, the plan was to move in with the family for the summer and help him get the kids back into their home, since they were temporarily staying with Dennis' mother.

"I had no expected to fall in love with the children, who so desperately needed someone," Yaklich said. "They were grieving for their mother, so I couldn't bear to leave them."

Barbara had died on Valentine's Day, and had "appeared fine" as her children left for school that morning. However, an hour later, Barbara was dead – and Dennis was the only person who had been with her as she died. According to some reports, there are members of the community who do continue to question Dennis' involvement in the death of his first wife, including at least one of his former co-workers.

"Dennis' fellow officers knew he was out of control, but they also knew when they needed him he would be the first to go through the door," Yaklich said. "No one who worked with him would go against him."

It was this feeling of hopelessness that eventually led Yaklich to hire gunmen to kill her husband, in an effort to finally end the ongoing abuse. She'd moved in with Dennis when she was only 22 and he was 30. The children were aged 3, 9, 11, and 12 – and she immediately fell into the role of step-mother, despite the abuse which began only a month after Yaklich moved in. She said she attempted to leave a few times, but always went back.

"I feared Dennis, but at the same time I felt at home with him because I had grown up in an abusive environment," Yaklich said. "I fell into the trap of thinking if I could make everything perfect for him, he wouldn't get mad at me or at the kids. Dennis' threats to kill me or kill someone I loved if I ever left again kept me there."

Dennis even threatened to use his access to federal law enforcement agents against Yaklich, telling her that she'd never be able to get away from him – these agents were capable of fiding anyone, anywhere. Eventually, she said, "I lost myself. I lost hope."

"I became very depressed and mad at myself because I had no trusted my instincts about leaving the relationship when the abuse started," Yaklich said. "Suicidal thoughts became an answer. Then came homicidal thoughts."

Looking back, Yaklich admitted that she wished she had listened to those first instincts, but eventually came to a point where she no longer cared. However, she said she has been working on bettering herself since being convicted and sentenced.

"Being in prison is similar to the prison I put myself in while I was married to Dennis," she said. "However, prison is also what you make of it, so I've enrolled in educational programs, had therapy, and also taken care of myself. Things I should have done in society."

A professional abuser

At a menacing 6'5" and 280 pounds, Dennis Yaklich was a competitive weightlifter who continuously used steroids to supplement his workouts – despite the fact that they also enhanced his aggressive tendencies. While the officers who worked with him conceded that he was always the go-to guy for breaking down a door or clearing a room, he was difficult to manage. In fact, when he did become confrontational, even a supervisor threatened to shoot him because they had no other way to defend themselves.

A former partner once stated that he felt he always had to "clean up after Dennis," and other co-workers have admitted they "dreaded" working with Dennis, because of his aggressive and unpredictable behaviour. Some of his closest colleagues have even confessed that Dennis displayed some "abusive tactics" on the job – while denying the complaints of citizens against him.

Yaklich endured what can only be described as domestic terrorism. While the physical abuse, which included slapping, choking, kicking, and pushing her down stairs as well as sadistic sexual assaults, was indeed disabling and troubling, the psychological abuse was almost worse. According to Yaklich, the threat of death loomed constantly – Dennis would put his gun to her head and threaten to kill her, point his finger at her in the shape of a gun and blow on it after miming shooting her with it, and even beating her under the cover of darkness so she wouldn't be able to prepare for the blows.

The physical abuse has been corroborated by a number of independent witnesses, including a mailman who reported seeing bruises on Yaklich's face, and a telephone repairman who had been called in twice to fix phones after Dennis had yanked them out of the wall in a fit of rage.

Following Yaklich's arrest, the repairman spoke with detectives investigating Dennis' death and said the bruises he had seen on Yaklich's neck and cheek were so prominent, he noticed them "at a glance." The detective inquired how the repairman could recall the incident so vividly, and he admitted that in his line of work, he sees "a lot of things like that in the low income areas and the projects, but I was shocked to see a cop's wife all bruised up like she was."

Cries unheard

Yaklich's first documented attempt for police intervention came in 1982, when she called Dennis' partner to explain that Dennis was "out of control" and threatening to kill her. The detective advised her to leave right away, but she said she was too afraid – if she left, she said, Dennis had told her he would kill her entire family, starting with her father.

Believing that Yaklich was in fear for her life, the detective immediately went to inform his supervisor about the call he'd received about his partner. According to the detective, the supervisor had gestured to indicate that he should just forget the call – it was none of their business – and the incident went unreported.

It was then that Yaklich realized that trying to get help from the police would be completely futile, and she would need to seek support elsewhere.

The next year, in November of 1983, Yaklich endured a short and traumatic visit with a psychologist. After Yaklich "sobbed uncontrollably" through the entire session, the psychologist recommended she leave her husband – but failed to offer her suggestions to muster the courage needed to do so, or what steps she could take to do it safely.

Since Yaklich was required to provide her abusive husband with detailed accounts of where she spent all her time, there was no way for her to continue therapy with regular appointments. She never went back for another session.

A few months later, Yaklich escaped to a battered women's shelter in Denver, in February of 1984. Dennis pleaded with her to come home, and even went so far as to promise that he would try to change – and because she was ashamed to go back to him again, Yaklich told the counselors that she was leaving the state.

Still, the abuse hadn't stopped another year later. Early in 1985, Yaklich tried talking to friends and family members – telling them she needed advice because Dennis was going to kill her. These claims were shrugged off by everyone she turned to, and the abuse began to escalate.

Feeling as though she had no other options, Yaklich began looking for an opportunity to kill herself. Her attempts failed, however, when she realized she would be abandoning her young son and step-children with their abusive father – and after witnessing the struggles of Barbara's children as they grieved the loss of their mother, she was unable to force that situation on her own child.

Later that year, the Pueblo Sheriff's Department received a 911 call from Yaklich's mother. One of the step-children had called Yaklich's parents after hearing what they thought was Dennis pushing Yaklich through a plate glass window. While it turned out that the noise was caused by just a bowl hitting the floor, the officers who responded barely acknowledged Yaklich.

In fact, their inspection of the situation involved a brief conversation with Dennis followed by a tour of the gym Dennis was building on the property. The situation only reinforced Yaklich's desperate situation on the other side of the blue line – living in fear of an abusive spouse with no support or protection from the authorities.

Finally, on December 12, 1985, one of Yaklich's friends finally responded to her pleas for help. A neighbour, Eddie Greenwell, waited at the Yaklich family's farm with his younger brother, Charles, into the early morning hours. When Dennis returned home after working a night shift, the brothers shot and killed him. Yaklich was inside the house, sleeping.

According to court documents, Yaklich had "approached several people" in an attempt to have her husband killed, and had met with Eddie Greenwell many times over a period of eight months. The Greenwell brothers were paid $4,200 in installments after the murder was committed – although the brothers testified they had been promised $45,000.

The story of the tragic marriage was detailed in a made-for-television movie called *Cries Unheard: The Donna Yaklich Story*. The film was released in 1994 and starred former Charlie's Angel Jaclyn Smith as Yaklich.

A disturbing conflict of interest

After Dennis was killed, the Pueblo Police Department – Dennis' employer – carried out an investigation into his death, despite the fact that the murder actually took place in the jurisdiction of the Pueblo Sheriff's Office. Lead roles in the inquiry were awarded to narcotics detectives – Dennis' partners.

The District Attorney was also a personal friend of Dennis', and even admitted to being a material witness in his own case. At the time of the trial, DA Sandstrom was wrapped up in a highly contested election – and this clear political agenda, combined with the attempts of the police department to hide its role in Yaklich's abuse and ultimately, Dennis' death, indicate incredible prejudice against Yaklich from the very beginning.

Not that Yaklich was surprised. After attempting to secure the help of police several times during the course of her abusive marriage, it was obvious to Yaklich that law enforcement was not on her side.

Still, the jury acquitted Yaklich of the charge of first-degree murder. Several jurors even thought Yaklich deserved to be acquitted of all charges, but felt intimidated by the Pueblo Police Department – and feared potential retaliation. Instead, the jury voted guilty on the charge of conspiracy to commit murder, believing that the fair-minded judge would give the battered wife the minimum sentence of eight years.

The probation supervisor who had conducted Yaklich's pre-sentencing investigation testified that Yaklich would be an "excellent candidate" for sentencing alternatives outside of the Department of Corrections, and gave the court his recommendation for the minimum sentence. His testimony affirmed the sense of desperation Yaklich claimed to be struggling with.

"I really felt that whether they did what she wanted done, to have Dennis killed, or whether Dennis found out and killed her, it didn't matter," he said. "She was at a point in her life where either was satisfactory."

However, the late Judge Seavy who presided over the trial chose to overlook the circumstances leading to Dennis' murder and remanded Yaklich to the Department of Corrections for a sentence of forty years. According to the judge, Yaklich "started this whole scenario," and therefore deserved to serve a period of time "in excess of the longest Greenwell's sentence."

"We cannot overlook the fact that Yaklich's participation in the death of her husband was not merely peripheral," stated court documents. "Had it not been for Yaklich, the Greenwells would not have been involved in this murder. Thus, in our view, we would be establishing poor public policy if Yaklich were to escape punishment by virtue of an unprecedented application of self-defense while the Greenwells were convicted of murder."

Still, the jurors were shocked and horrified by the severity of Judge Seavy's harsh sentence. More than half of the serving jurors submitted letters expressing their disappointment with the resulting sentence to a judge who presided over Yaklich's sentencing reconsideration a few years later. These letters were dismissed by that judge, however, who felt "that they must not allow for personal sympathy to influence their decision." Several of the jurors who served on the initial trial event went on to diligently advocate for Yaklich's early release, eighteen years later.

According to Dr. Lenore Walker, who counseled and evaluated Yaklich and provided expert testimony at her trial, Judge Seavy was "using the court and a woman's life to express his own ignorance of a battered woman's plight."

The conspiracy

According to court documents, Yaklich did receive payments totalling more than $250,000 under her late husband's three life insurance policies – leading to a theory that the motivation that pushed her to arrange her husband's death was to obtain this insurance money. The defense argued that Yaklich suffered from "battered woman syndrome," and that the conspiracy to commit murder was a "justifiable act of self-defence ... committed under duress resulting from years of physical and psychological battering by her husband."

"Yaklich lived in a constant state of fear of her husband," the defense argued. "At the time of his death, she believed she was in imminent danger of being killed by him or receiving great bodily injury from him."

The defense went on to explain that many battered women are unable to safely leave their abusive spouses – and in fact, the abuse often escalates as a result of a separation. Abusers have also been known to pursue their victims after they've left, subjecting them to "brutal attacks."

"Additionally, battered women may not psychologically or emotionally have the alternative of leaving the abuser because of their low self-esteem, their emotional and economic dependency, the absence of another place to go, and the woman's legitimate fear of the abuser's response to her leaving," stated the defense. "Battered women become trapped in their own fear and often feel that their only recourse is to kill the batterer or be killed."

Several people involved with the case, including District Attorney Sandstrom, have stated that if Yaklich had gone ahead and committed the murder herself, "she would have walked." However, the DA and many others also question the validity of Yaklich's testimony, including that Dennis was abusing her – maintaining the theory that Yaklich conspired to have him killed just to receive the insurance money.

The DA even stated that "if she had shot him herself, there would be no issue" – leading some to wonder if Sandstrom sees money as an acceptable motive for murder, as long as you follow through with it on your own.

Like most battered women, Yaklich both loved and hated her husband. Killing him herself would have been difficult, as she was afraid that as soon as she pointed a gun at him to save herself and her children, the love she had for him would "override her fear of him," and cause her to second-guess her decision. The ramifications from that could have bene deadly.

Another concern for Yaklich was her husband's established persona of invincibility – one he had carefully instilled in her over years of repeated psychological and physical abuse. Not only did Yaklich struggle to trust in her own ability to kill her husband, she struggled to believe that he would ever really die.

One of the prosecution's expert witnesses, Dr. Alice Brill, said in her testimony that Yaklich didn't meet the traditional profile of a battered woman. These women, according to Brill, generally kill their spouses with little premeditation and show little interest in pursuing relationships with other men – while Yaklich spent at least ten months planning her husband's murder, and had had at least one extramarital affair about a year before Dennis was killed.

Dennis' children also continue to question Yaklich's testimony, stating that none of them had ever witnessed any physical abuse from Dennis during the eight years of the couple's marriage. After Yaklich's parole hearing in October 2005, Dennis' daughter Vanessa fought back tears while talking about the court's decision to release Yaklich after she'd only served eighteen years of her forty-year sentence.

"It's devastating – I don't believe justice has prevailed," she said. "My father died at age 38. He was stripped of his opportunity to live life. He was prevented from raising his children, from seeing us grow up and accomplishing our goals."

Vanessa stated that Yaklich's claims of beatings and abuse were "an outright lie" – and that the depiction of the family's life shown in the TV-movie *Cries Unheard* were based entirely on prison interviews with Yaklich herself, with no supporting evidence or facts contributed by other relatives or friends.

Vanessa added that just two months before her father was killed, Yaklich had told her that Dennis had asked for a divorce – but that the couple planned to delay the proceedings until after the Christmas holidays, for the sake of the younger children. This story has been corroborated by Dennis' brother, who said Dennis told him over the phone that he planned to divorce Yaklich once the holidays had passed.

"(Dennis') life was taken because he was going to divorce my step-mother and not because she was the victim of abuse," Vanessa said. "I never feared my father, nor did I observe any abuse, whether it be psychological or physical, perpetrated by him. His demeanor was calm and loving, his words encouraging and supportive. I can honestly state my step-mother did not provide my siblings or myself with the same."

According to Vanessa, Yaklich didn't show any grief or remorse after Dennis had been killed – and even slapped Vanessa when she began to cry at her father's funeral. She went on to detail the ongoing "injustice," claiming to defend her father since he is no longer able to defend himself.

"My stepmother's legal defense was paid for by my father's life insurance proceeds and my family and I believe she profited from the made-for-television monstrosity," Vanessa said. "Most recently, her financial status has provided her with the ability to hire a media publicist."

Questions also remain about the relationship Yaklich had with her defense attorney, John Giduck. Records show Giduck and Yaklich took a romantic vacation to Jamaica together prior to her arrest in March 1986 – a getaway funded entirely from the death benefit Yaklich received after having her husband murdered.

In fact, the vacation was cut short when Yaklich was notified of the charges that were being brought against her, and surrendered to police upon her return to Pueblo. Most of the insurance money had already been spent by the time Yaklich was arrested.

According to information reported in the Colorado Springs Gazette, Yaklich had been involved in an extramarital affair about a year before Dennis' murder, and had begun a romantic relationship with Giduck only weeks after her husband's death. Giduck had apparently attended Dennis' funeral, where he had given Yaklich his business card and told him to call if she needed anything.

Yaklich reached out to him a few days later, after police asked her to verify the statement she'd given with a routine polygraph test.

A safe and abuse-free life

Still, Yaklich had a spotless record prior to her incarceration, which continued even after she was sent to prison – a testament to her strength of character. According to prison records, Yaklich managed to vigilantly avoid conflict and strictly followed the many rules surrounding prison life. Despite being forced into an environment filled with trouble, Yaklich managed to stay out of it through her entire eighteen-year term.

During her incarceration, Yaklich obtained an associate's degree as well as a Bachelor's degree in psychology – while working in maintenance and then in a computer-refurbishing program at the correctional facility. According to staff there, Yaklich was a hard and industrious worker, even volunteering her time as a member of the Fire Response Team, comprised of prisoners trained in firefighting and first aid.

Yaklich has also volunteered with several programs that support victims of abuse, earning high praise from her Department of Corrections supervisors regarding the effectiveness of her work with young people. She encourages victims of domestic abuse to seek support from therapy groups to find the strength to break away from an abusive partner – to learn how to stay away emotionally and physically.

"Educating ourselves about the issues and statistics relative to domestic violence will help us pass this information on to the next generation," Yaklich said. "Our children need to learn that they have the right to safe and abuse-free lives."

HUSBAND KILLER MICHELLE REYNOLDS

55

GARY GUIDEN

On July 5th, 2004, a Frito Lay delivery pulled into the empty parking lot of a distribution center in Rome, Georgia. The man noticed that another man- one he didn't recognize- was coming out of the office, and although someone in the office in the early morning hours wasn't unusual, not recognizing the man was. According to the diver, the man who came into view appeared to be nervous- looking over his shoulder, glancing around, and checking behind him.

The man, possibly unaware of the delivery driver still sitting in his vehicle, exits the building and enters a mini-van after removing his shirt. Thinking this was odd, the delivery driver entered the Frito Lay office only to discover the scene of a horror film.

He discovered the slumped over body of the regional manager, Thad Reynolds, sitting in a pool of his own blood. He called 911 and EMT's and police officers responded within minutes. However, it was too late. Thad Reynolds was dead before anyone arrived.

Ross Cavitt, a reporter at the scene, noted that Reynolds had been stabbed 19 times. Due to the nature of the stab wounds and the amount of blood, it was obvious to Cavitt that there had been a great struggle.

Thad's death sent shock through his community, but hit his church, the Hollywood Baptist, the hardest as Thad and his wife Michelle were well-known within the church community. In her early days, Michelle had been popular in high school and well respected within her community.

Thad, on the other hand, was a dedicated Christian and devoted father to his 4 children, as well as a loving husband to his wife, Michelle. As a young man, Thad had been heavily involved in sports and was popular at his high school.

"He could always make your day better" stated Julie Crumbley about her late friend Thad.

Michelle was a mother of 4 and a likeable person, according to Thad's close friend, Julie Crumbley.

Before becoming a mother, Michelle had worked as an administrative assistant, but had given the job up after giving birth to her first child in 1992. After the couple began to have children, the decision was made that Michelle would be a stay at home mom and raise their children.

In 1995, however, the couple's relationship took a turn for the worse and Michelle asked for a divorce. Thad's sister, Beverly Owners, claims that Michelle hadn't been happy just being a mother and a wife. It's been said that Michelle had made the following comment to a pastor at the couple's church: "You put your wife on a pedestal, but Thad never put me on a pedestal."

Thad agreed to the divorce, but regretted his decision as he didn't believe in divorce or broken homes. Undone by the divorce, Thad turned to his church for help. Two years after their divorce, the couple remarried, built a new home, and added more children to their family.

Thad's career began to flourish, after he was hired into the Frito Lay company where he was able to work his way to district manager. He also sang in the church's choir and served as a deacon, as well as helped other couples with marriage counseling.

"They appeared to be the most perfect family whenever you would see them" says Crumbley.

Thad's mother told Dateline that the couple had been called Barbie and Ken because of how well their life seemed to be going.

Both Michelle and Thad had a passion for children and worked with the church's youth group to put on shows, skits, and performances in various locations. They worked closely with the church's youth minister, Scott Harper and his wife, Paige. Thad and Scott became best friends and the families became joined at the hip. Paige and Michelle also became close, bonding over their stay at home lifestyles and busy husbands.

So, what went wrong? The answer to this was revealed only after a shocking truth involving Michelle and her best friend's husband came to light.

In 2004, Thad decided to become a minister, as he felt that God was calling to him to join the ministry. In June of that year, Michelle signed up to help the Harper family with a youth retreat, but called Paige shortly before they were set to leave and said that she had had a change of heart.

"She called me last minute and said that she was going to book her own room and was not going to room with me, because she needed her own time" says Paige, when asked about the phone call. This meant that Michelle would be the only chaperon who had her own private room.

"Michelle was distant. She wouldn't speak to me or look me in the eye" Paige says. Paige grew concerned and confronted her best friend. "I said "Michelle is there something wrong? Have I done something to offend you?" and she looked me in the eye and said no, I just want to be around people who are on fire for God.""

As her husband prepared to become a minister, Michelle began to spend less time with Paige and more time with her husband, Scott.

"She would constantly be asking him for assistance. More and more she would ask him for help working with the children or how to do certain things with them. They began to email and communicate" says prosecutor, Leigh Patterson.

On Saturday, July 3rd, 2004, the Harper and Reynolds' met up for a long weekend celebration. The next day, a Sunday, the met up once again to attend church together. That day, the families met at a local park to play volleyball, gave snacks, and enjoy each other's company.

"I noticed Michelle being kind of flirtatious towards other men, asking somebody to help her throw a football and stuff like that." Paige says.

"She was a little bit too flirty...wanting other men to pay attention to her" agrees Patterson.

Despite Michelle's odd behavior at the picnic, she and her husband loaded up their children at the end of the evening and went home like nothing had happened.

The next morning Thad left for work before sunrise and while Michelle and the kids were still asleep. After only a few minutes at the office, a van pulled up outside of the office where Thad was working. The driver was Scott Harper, and within a few minutes, Thad would be dead on the floor of his office.

On July 5th, when Thad's body was discovered, the city of Rome, Georgia was thrown into chaos.

The first question on investigator's lips was who would launch a violent attack on the well-loved church deacon?

"There were wounds all over his body, including defensive wounds" says Patterson.

The only witness had been the delivery driver who had discovered Thad's body, but he had been unable to get a good look at Thad's attacker's face or the license plate of the van he had been driving.

Upon investigation of the scene, it became apparent to police that Thad had managed to wound his attacker. This was proved by a large amount of blood that was found by the office doorway- blood that matched up with the delivery driver's statement claiming that the unknown man stopped by the door before getting into his van and leaving the scene.

Also on the scene, police found the empty case for a hunting knife and a pair of glasses. The glasses also matched up with witness testimony, as the man was seen removing his shirt and in doing so, his glasses could have fallen off and been left behind in his haste to get away.

Scott Harper was called to help identify Thad's body and was one of the first people to learn of his death. Scott called his wife and upon hearing the news, Paige become worried about Michelle.

The Harpers drove to the Reynolds house to be with Michelle, however, upon arrival, they found that the church's head pastor was already there.

According to family and friends, Michelle has taken the news stoically.

"You would think that when we got there, Michelle would come and give us a hug or cry and she didn't" said Beverly Owens, surprised at how Michelle took the news.

Thad's mother also noticed Michelle's lack of outward emotion and was concerned by it.

"She had just bought a black dress about two weeks before and made the comment "whoever thought that I'd be using it for this.""

Meanwhile, back at the crime scene, investigators had begun to wonder about Thad's death. To them, it didn't appear to be a random attack and robbery situation, but seemed to have been calculated and planned, as Thad's murderer didn't take any of his money or anything that he had had on him. The reason behind the attack appeared to be one thing: to kill Thad Reynolds.

On the news that evening, a clue was unearthed as to who could have killed the deacon. Scott Roberts, a coworker of Scott Harper, had heard the news asking for leads and picked up the phone almost immediately.

Roberts called the police department and reported to the officials that his coworker, Scott Harper was both friends with Thad and drove a burgundy minivan like the one that had been witnessed leaving the crime scene.

Roberts was asked for a statement and while telling them what he knew, he alerted the police that Scott Harper had been having an affair with someone- information that he claimed he had stumbled upon without meaning to. Roberts worked with phonelines and was tasked with fixing them. A few weeks before the murder, he had tapped into a conversation to fix the phoneline and overheard Harper talking to a woman who wasn't his wife, Paige. He had also overheard that the woman's name was Michelle.

"They were flirting. Lover chit chat, if you will. Kind of reminded me of high school sweethearts" said Roberts in an interview with Dateline.

Officials ended their interview with Roberts by asking a simple question- did Harper wear glasses? Roberts had answered that, yes, Scott Harper did wear glasses.

This left police to wonder were the connections between the van, the glasses, and a possible affair all just coincidence? Or was there something sinister going on?

The Harpers were then brought in for official questioning, where Scott told investigators that he had hurt his hand at the gym, when he was asked why his hand was bandaged. This explained his hand but didn't explain why his glasses were missing.

Scott was released, despite police not believing his story. Paige was starting to doubt her husband, as well.

"When we left the station, I asked him if he knew anything about Thad's murder...about what was going on" Paige said "and he said "do you realize what you're asking me?""

Police obtained a warrant to search Scott's computer at the hospital that he worked at, in hopes of getting answers. They had a particular interest to look into Scott's emails, as they were saved on a public server and could be easily accessed.

It was found that a large portion of the emails were to and from Thad's wife, Michelle. At first, the emails were innocent- mostly consisting of routine topics such as the youth group that Michelle worked with at the church. Gradually, though, the emails became more personal and revealing in nature.

About a month before the death of her husband, the tone of the emails changed.

"She was coming onto him in the emails. Usually under the guise of I know I shouldn't feel this way" Patterson says, referring to Michelle and the emails that she sent to Scott "and he fell for it."

"The emails, especially toward the end, were very graphic and specific" said prosecutor Natalee Staats.

It wasn't clear from the emails when their affair became physical, however, records show that at the youth retreat in June, Scott had booked Michelle's room and stayed in it with her. Paige, although quiet about the whole thing, had noticed Scott get up and leave the room and noted that he didn't return until the next morning.

"He had gone down to Michelle's room and even though they were on a church trip with kids and his wife, and Michelle's daughter there as a participant, they had continued their affair" said Patterson.

Police combed over every detail of their emails, but couldn't decide whether Michelle had coaxed Scott into murdering her husband or not. According to Patterson, Michelle had been very careful with what she said and how she said it.

"Michelle never said "I need you to kill my husband" said Staats. However, she hinted at the idea by sayings things like "You'll have to live longer than Thad for us to be together because he'll never agree to divorce."

After Michelle had planted the idea in Scott's head, he had gone on to lookup poison and arsenic, as well an essay on how to commit the perfect murder Patterson reported.

On the evening of July 4th, hours before the murder would happen, the two exchanged a final round of emails.

"The night before, she tells him what Thad's schedule was going to be the next morning. Specific directions of where he was going to be" she also reports.

"Those were all glaring clues to the police that Michelle might have been involved in a conspiracy to murder her husband" said Staats, in agreeance with Patterson.

Scott had sent Michelle an email giving her an out. The email told Michelle to tell him if she had any hesitations, and that if she did, he wouldn't go through with it. Michelle replied that didn't have any hesitations and was ready for the event to take place.

Scott Harper was charged with murder on July 8th, 2004 after he turned himself in. He was charged with murder, felony murder, aggravated assault, and aggravated battery.

Authorities hoped that Scott would tie Michelle into the case, however, Scott was blinded by his feelings for her and was willing to protect her at all costs. He invoked the right to remain silent and didn't make another statement for or against Michelle's innocence.

Michelle was also arrested, as police had enough evidence from Michelle's own emails, that she had been involved.

"Once they figured it out, they decided pretty quickly that they had enough to charge her as well" said Michelle's attorney, Jim Berry.

An hour or so after Scott had turned himself in, Michelle was placed under arrest and brought into police custody and like her lover, Michelle refused to talk.

"Michelle was arrested as she came out of her attorney's office in downtown Rome" said Patterson.

"I had no clue. Everybody seemed happy" said Paige, who was shocked by the news that Michelle and Scott were in custody.

"Friends that they interacted with at the church didn't dream that the family pastor was having an affair with the deacon's wife" Patterson said.

The fact that Michelle and Scott could and would conspire to murder Thad Reynolds was unthinkable to the members of the church, who knew both people as being kind and good-hearted.

Scott Roberts, after hearing the news, took it upon himself to search the hospital where he and Scott worked for anything that police might have missed. He focused on the IT department's data center and more specifically, he focused on the tile floor. He was able to lift up a tile using a suction cup, and underneath, found the item that would be pinned as the murder weapon: a hunting knife. He also discovered a pile of bloody clothes.

In November, 4 months after Thad's murder, Michelle and Scott were summoned to the court room for a preliminary hearing to decide who would be tried first.

"The state gets to elect, by law, who to try first. We had elected to try her first" said Patterson. The decision to try Michelle first was a risk, as her case was the weaker of the two. Prosecutors knew that she hadn't bene the one to physically take Thad's life, however, they held her responsible for the murder.

"She was the person that made it happen" said Ross Cavitt "even though Scott Harper had the murder weapon in his hand, they could see that he was following orders from Michelle which made her ultimately responsible for the crime."

The emails, although suspicious, didn't pin Michelle to giving the orders, but prosecutors hoped that Harper would. They hoped that by presenting him with the evidence that was quickly stacking against him, they would be able to convince him to cut a deal and turn his back on Michelle.

Aside from the leverage of evidence that prosecutors had, the DA had written and notified the court that she would be seeking the death penalty for both Scott and Michelle.

"After the death of a fine young man, a father of four, to seek the death penalty wasn't that surprising" said Cavitt, in regard to the DA's email.

All that was left for prosecutors to do was wait and hope that Scott would cave.

"I had begged Scotty to do what was needed and to give up the information, and to tell the story of his involvement and Michelle's involvement" Paige told Dateline "and he would always tell me no, to just leave her out of this"

"He was smitten and head over heels in love with her" Cavitt said.

"I think that she couldn't have cared less about him. I think he was just the muscle behind the act" said Patterson, who was convinced that Michelle had simply used Harper's infatuation with her to get him to do her bidding.

Despite the prosecutor's hopes, Harper continued to clam up when it came to Michelle's involvement. It seemed that even the threat of the death penalty wasn't enough to get him to talk.

Years passed this way.

"Meetings with him resulted in nothing. He would not come forward" said Staats.

Finally, in the fall of 2008 and 4 years after both parties had been locked behind bars, Scott was ready to cooperate with prosecutors.

Scott's attorneys helped him decide on a deal and upon this conversation, it became to clear to everyone involved that Harper was still infatuated with Michelle as his concern for her took center stage. He would take a life sentence and plead guilty, as long as the death penalty was taken off of Michelle's case. He did, however, agree to testify at Michelle's trial.

"He effectively saved and betrayed her at the same time" said one of his attorneys.

In the court room on October 1st, 2008, Harper sat with prosecutors and told them his account of Thad's death.

"He told us that he still loved her and he was going to do anything in his power to minimize her involvement" said Patterson

"Michelle had basically said that Thad would not leave easily. He would fight for her and not give up on their marriage and that it would get ugly" said another of his attorneys "and he said that he could deal with ugly."

After this conversation, according to Scott, he had purchased the hunting knife and the next day, he had had lunch with Michelle. The two had parked and kissed in the back seat like a pair of teenagers, and it was during this time that Michelle had asked him if he had talked to her husband yet. When he told her that he hadn't, Michelle withdrew her affection and became cold and distant towards him.

Scott said that he had been afraid of losing her, so four days later he had woken up before dawn and driven to the Frito Lay distribution center with the intent to deal with Thad Reynolds.

As he entered the building, Thad had looked up and asked him what he was doing there. Scott Harper had replied with "I want what you got."

Harper's story was not enough to pin the murder on Michelle: it was only enough to charge her with adultery.

"All it would take was for one person on the jury to say that okay. Maybe Michelle really did think that Scott was just going to talk to her husband" Patterson said.

On January 13th, 2010, Michelle was brought back into court after 6 years of being in jail. The officials and attorneys present had been expecting for Harper to testify against Michelle, however, this did not happen. Michelle stood before the jury and plead guilty to voluntary manslaughter.

"Getting Scott Harper's statement was like pulling teeth and she didn't think we'd get it. That's the only reason that she plead guilty"

" She knew that she was responsible for the death, in some way, because of the affair and because of that she felt that she should plead guilty to something" said Scott's attorney.

At the hearing that day, Thad's mother asked Michelle why her son had had to die for this.

"There was no response" said Thad's mother, Kittie Walker, "her eyes were just cold. No remorse, no feelings, nothing."

"She knew that Thad would not have let her take the kids away" said Beverly Owens "and she knew that that was the only way to get him out of the picture"

In the end, she was sentenced to 20 years behind bars, with credit being given to the time she had already served in county jail. Until her release, Michelle is unable to see her children and will lose custody of them.

According to Scott Roberts, there were people who upon hearing her sentencing, didn't feel as if justice had been served.

"I would have liked to see Michelle get a lot more time for it. I would have liked to see her life in prison" said Kittie Walker.

Many people in Rome, Georgia agreed that although Scott had wielded the knife, Michelle was the villain behind the plot.

"We're in a religious town and I think that many people believed that Scotty had been manipulated by her and that she was the devil incarnate" said Jim Berry.

Despite the tension and hard feelings, Paige Harper was visibly shaken by the case.

"Scott and Michelle were the two most important people in my life other than my kids, so for this to happen...it really makes me wonder how well I know people" she said.

In the aftermath of the murder, Thad's mother got custody of the kids and Paige divorced her husband in 2005. Despite writing letters in the early days of their sentences, Michelle and Scott have stopped communicating.

Within recent years, Michelle has written to officials asking why she isn't allowed to see her children.

"We do it all the time with adults- no contact with whomever. That's not anything new. That's a standard law order in nearly every murder case I've had, even if they're in the same family" responded Patterson, who also stated that Michelle is well aware of this order as it was part of her plea deal back in January of 2010.

Judge J. Bryant Durham, who had found Michelle guilty in years prior, mentioned that once her children turn 18 they can visit her in prison. Currently, this means that Michelle's eldest daughter, 22-year old Alisan and her infant grandchild can visit her in prison whenever they wish.

"Like it or not, if she decides to go over there every day, I don't think that can be stopped" Durham told Patterson.

The intent of the order was to restrict visitation until Michelle was released, however, due to lack of specifics and bad wording, the age of visitation remains 18.

There's no question that a good man died for less than good reasons, but there are still questions in the minds of his family and friends. Why had it happened? Had death really been Michelle's only option? It's up for speculation and, unfortunately, no one will ever know for sure.

KILLING THE WRONG MAN : THE TRUE STORY OF LEE ANN REIDEL

69

ANITA MURDOCK

What could lead a normal middle class woman to be accused of killing an innocent man? This is the story of convicted murderer Lee Ann Reidel.

Early Years

Lee Ann Reidel, then Lee Ann Armanini, was born in the summer of 1967. Her childhood was very normal. She was the second of four children, to parents David and Pat Armanini. The family lived in a middle class, suburban area in Long Island, New York. Things went well for a few years; they went on regular vacations and spent the holidays together, life was good.

It was when Lee Ann turned 11 that things started to go wrong. Her parents divorced. Pat Armanini, Lee Ann's mother, moved to Florida to live with a new female lover. Lee Ann was left behind in New York. From that point she was raised by her father, David Armanini, who later remarried. Unsurprisingly, these difficult circumstances seemed to have a negative effect on Lee Ann's life and she entered a downward spiral.

Her teenage years were troubled, culminating in a failed marriage at the young age of 19. As a result of this marriage Lee Ann had her first child, a son named Christopher. Lee Ann raised Christopher alone and had the typical struggles of a young, single mother. The main worry was money; some claim that financial insecurities during this period of Lee Ann's life affected her later actions. However, despite some tough times, David Armanini, Lee Ann's father, claims that she was a responsible mother, who put the needs of her son first.

Family Life

The following years passed without incident. Lee Ann didn't have another serious boyfriend until she met Paul Reidel in 1998. The pair met at a Long Island gym where Lee Ann had started working out. They quickly fell in love. Friends of Lee Ann claim that she was very happy. She liked Paul Reidel because he was a strong, muscly man who could protect her, but he also had a gentle nature. The relationship progressed quickly, and soon they were engaged. Cathy Armanini, Lee Ann's stepmother, stated that the family were very pleased when they discovered that the pair had plans to marry.

Paul Reidel had a difficult past – he spent several years in prison on drug dealing charges when he was 19. However, he had since reformed and become a very ambitious man. He opened a business named Dolphin Fitness Club, with his best friend, Alex Algeri. Dolphin Fitness Club in Amityville, New York, was a popular 24 hour gym for weightlifters. The business was thriving and Paul was doing very well financially. Lee Ann appreciated her new lifestyle – she had gone from being a struggling single mother, to the partner of a rich business owner.

Lee Ann and Paul had a church wedding in July 1998. The wedding was quite a lavish display, with impressive decorations and catering. Guests described it as a beautiful fairy tale wedding. No one would ever have predicted the terrible events that were soon to follow.

Marriage Troubles

Not long after they were married, Lee Ann discovered that she was pregnant with her second child. Again, family members were delighted. From the outside everything seemed perfect. However, the stress of owning a 24 hour business and the prospect of being a father was starting to get to Paul. He had started using drugs again and quickly became addicted to crack cocaine.

Pat Armanini, Lee Ann's mother, claims that Lee Ann confided in her about Reidel's drug use and that she was very distressed by it. A number of incidents took place involving Lee Ann driving around during the night, trying to locate Paul and bring him back home. Pat Armanini stated that on one occasion Lee Ann even followed him to the location of a drug deal in order to prevent it from happening. This all happened while Lee Ann was heavily pregnant. Lee Ann wanted to preserve their relationship and help Paul get off drugs. Her mother believes that she thought the new baby would fix things between them, and be the wake-up call that Paul needed to stop taking crack cocaine.

For a short time, this did seem to be the case. Paul became very excited about the idea of having a child, especially when he found out it was a boy. When the child was born, they called him Nicholas. Paul asked his best friend and business partner, Alex Algeri, to be Nicholas' godfather. Algeri happily agreed.

However, despite a happy period, Paul Reidel's drugs habits remained. He continued to use crack cocaine regularly. Lee Ann would apparently find needles and vials around the house, and feared that their small child would end up getting injured or worse. In July 2000, things came to ahead and Paul returned home from work one night to find that Lee Ann, his new born baby and stepson, were gone. Also missing was a large amount of money and possessions from the house. Lee Ann had fled to her mother's place in Florida with the children, taking $120000 with her.

Losing his family seemed to be the wake-up call that Paul Reidel needed. He was afraid that he would no longer be able to see his son. Reidel hired a lawyer to help fight for shared custody of Nicholas and he wanted Lee Ann and the baby to come back to New York while they waited for a custody decision. Paul stated that he wanted to be part of Nicholas' life, and he couldn't do that from so far away. Ultimately though, Reidel did not want his family to fall apart and he spent the next four months trying to reconcile with his wife. He made many promises to Lee Ann during this time. Most importantly, Reidel agreed to go to rehab and ditch his cocaine habit.

Lee Ann and the children eventually returned to Long Island in December 2000. It seemed like the two were trying to sort out their marriage and wanted to try again. Everyone believed that they had gotten over the difficult drugs issues and were now on the path towards happy family life once more. Paul was pleased, he was able to stay in the area of his business, and see his wife and son every day. However, not all was as it seemed and Lee Ann's motivations for returning to Long Island would later be called into question.

The Murder

One month later on the 17th January 2001, an unbelievable act of violence took place. Alex Algeri was shot in the face and killed outside the Dolphin Fitness Club. Gym members and the local community of Amityville were shocked; it was obviously a cold blooded murder.

Like any typical January in New York, the weather was very cold and there was a covering of snow on the ground. It was 7.20 in the evening and already dark. It was Paul Reidel's night off; Alex Algeri was covering the late shift at the gym. During what had so far been a perfectly normal evening, Alex popped out to get a CD from his car for one of the regular aerobics classes. He exited the building through the backdoor. The car park was not well lit and would have been very dark. He went round to the passenger side of the car to collect the CD from the glove compartment. Suddenly, a man jumped out of another vehicle parked nearby. As Algeri turned around, the man shot him several times in the face and neck.

Alex Algeri made it back into the gym trying to get help, but quickly collapsed and was dead before he arrived at hospital.

There was chaos. No one could understand why anyone would want Alex Algeri dead. The consensus was that Algeri was a friendly, popular individual who didn't have any known enemies. For a long time, the police had no leads in their investigation into the murder and people began to wonder if Algeri was really the intended victim.

Rumours spread that perhaps the killer had meant to shoot Paul Reidel instead. After all, Paul was the one with the criminal background. He had taken and dealt drugs for many years, and could have gotten involved with the wrong person. Maybe he had drug related debts, or someone was jealous of his flashy lifestyle. However, at this point there was no evidence that this was the case.

Lee Ann seemed to become panicked after Algeri's funeral. She apparently started asking Paul if it was supposed to be him, and what if she and the baby had been there – what if someone came to their house. Lee Ann convinced Paul that they might be in danger in New York, and that the family should move back to Florida.

Running Away

In 2001, the family did just this. Reidel, Lee Ann and the two children, Christopher and Nicholas, moved back to Florida permanently. Reidel was now the sole owner of the Dolphin Fitness Club and he wanted to remain in charge of the Long Island business. He decided to try and run things from Florida, flying out on regular business trips to check how everything was going. Lee Ann and Paul had plans to build a house for them and their two children in Florida. According to Lee Ann's friend, Mary Hanrahan, Lee Ann and Reidel were both very positive about the move. Reidel apparently spoke excitedly about their plans to build a property and yet again, everything appeared to be going fine for them.

The police in Long Island still had a murder investigation with no leads. Months passed without any new information on the case.

On one of Paul's many business trips to New York he received some unpleasant news from a relative. His relative claimed that every time Paul went out of town, a man went to see Lee Ann at the husband and wife's apartment in Florida. The suspicion was that Lee Ann was involved in an affair.

Reidel quickly dismissed the stories about Lee Ann being unfaithful. He believed that their relationship was stronger than ever because Lee Ann was pregnant again. He even told his relatives that the couple planned to call their new baby Paul, after him. Perhaps some family members had their doubts, but for several months everything went smoothly and Lee Ann and Reidel seemed content together.

A Lead

However, all that was about to change. In November 2001 police arrested a drug dealer in New York, named Michael Hubbard. Hubbard tipped off police that Ralph Salierno and Scott Paget from Florida were involved in the murder of Alex Algeri. Hubbard was trying to help the police and give them the impression that he was cooperating in the hope that his own drug dealing convictions would be dropped.

Police quickly brought in Salierno and Paget for questioning. From the very beginning Paget claimed that Salierno was the one who actually committed the murder and fired the gun at Algeri. Paget stated that he was just the driver. Salierno feigned ignorance about the murder for a while, but when he discovered that Paget had pointed the finger at him, he decided to offer his own rundown of events. In Salierno's story, Lee Ann was the one who came up with the plan to commit a murder, and Salierno was merely trying to follow her instructions.

Salierno confirmed that he and Lee Ann had been having an affair since the first time she moved to Florida in July 2000. Lee Ann's own mother, Pat Armanini, had introduced them, with the idea that Salierno could protect Lee Ann if Paul Reidel ever came to Florida and tried to take baby Nicholas. However, the relationship had developed into something much more. The two had fallen in love and kept seeing each other even when Lee Ann and Reidel were supposedly back together. Salierno claimed that Lee Ann had given him instructions to go to New York and kill Paul Reidel, offering him a potential payment of $100000. Salierno said that the killing of Alex Algeri was a case of mistaken identity.

Paul Reidel and Alex Algeri did not look dissimilar; they were both very strong, muscular men and had similar features. Obviously, they shared the same work place and even drove the same type of car. The murder had also taken place in the poorly lit gym carpark on a dark January evening. A case of mistaken identity did not seem impossible to police. Salierno's story was further backed up when he revealed that he was the father of Lee Ann's third child. This proved to be true, meaning that Lee Ann and Salierno had continued to see each other even after Alex Algeri's murder. So far, Salierno's version of events appeared to be adding up.

After Salierno admitted to killing Alex Algeri, Lee Ann confessed that she had indeed been having an affair with Salierno. The new baby, named Zachary, was his. However, she strongly denied that she had any part in planning her husband's murder. Lee Ann claimed that Salierno must have committed the murder in a fit of jealousy over the fact that the husband and wife appeared to be reconciling, and that Algeri was simply in the wrong place at the wrong time. Lee Ann also said that she had continued the affair with Salierno after Alex Algeri's death because her husband had changed – he was withdrawn and paranoid. She maintained that she had no idea that Salierno was the one who killed Algeri.

The police were put in a difficult situation – they were faced with numerous conflicting stories and very little physical evidence. They concluded that the only option was to let the case go to court and see what the outcome would be. In March 2003 Lee Ann Reidel was also arrested for the murder of Alex Algeri, it was decided that she and Salierno would be co-defendants.

The Trial

In March 2004, Lee Ann and Salierno were tried in the same room at Suffolk County courthouse, and faced the same prosecutors, but the outcome would be decided by two different juries. This is quite an unusual set up. The pair faced several charges including first degree murder, second degree murder and conspiracy to commit murder.

The prosecutor was Assistant District Attorney Denise Merrifield. Merrifield began by establishing that the intended victim was in fact, Paul Reidel, not Alex Algeri. Salierno confirmed this in his admission. The real question was did Salierno act alone, or was he acting on the instruction of Lee Ann?

Many witnesses were called upon during the trial. There was no physical evidence of Lee Ann's involvement so the prosecution relied heavily on the testimony of these witnesses. One notable testimony was from Lee Ann's mother's former lover, Elizabeth Russo. Russo claimed that she and Lee Ann's mother had initially introduced Lee Ann and Salierno with the intention of providing protection to Lee Ann. Salierno was told that if Paul Reidel came to Florida Salierno should threaten him and break his legs. This account suggested that Lee Ann was open to violent acts towards Paul Reidel. Russo clearly implied that she believed Lee Ann was capable of giving the instruction to Salierno to commit murder. Russo's account was particularly important for the prosecution because, unlike most of the other witnesses they called, she was not a criminal.

Scott Paget had already admitted that he drove Salierno back and forth to Long Island, New York on the night of the murder. Paget said that Salierno paid him $3000 dollars to drive the getaway car. He received a lower sentence of 18 years for cooperation with police. He also testified against Lee Ann – though the defence maintained that he could have simply been doing this in order to help his own case. Paget testified that Lee Ann instructed Salierno to kill Reidel. He said that Lee Ann gave Salierno a photograph of Reidel and told him the address of the Dolphin Fitness Club. Although this was a damning testimony, the defence tried to argue that Paget was not a reliable witness due to his own conviction and involvement in the case.

However, Lee Ann's case was damaged further when Michael Paglianti, a Florida drug dealer, was called to give his testimony. He said that he had been present when Lee Ann and Salierno met and discussed breaking Paul Reidel's legs. He also claimed that he had heard Lee Ann say that she wanted Reidel dead. Paglianti corroborated Paget's story by saying that he saw Lee Ann give a photograph of Reidel to Salierno. Finally, Paglianti testified that after the night of the murder and Algeri's funeral, Lee Ann verbally abused Salierno for killing the wrong guy.

Having heard from numerous witnesses, Lee Ann's case was not looking good. However, the defence pointed out that most of the witnesses were criminals and there was still no physical evidence of Lee Ann's guilt. There were some discrepancies with the car that Salierno and Paget drove to Long Island, with no record of who paid for the car, or where they rented it from. Lee Ann's attorney, Bruce Barket, questioned why Salierno had killed the wrong man. Surely, if he was acting on Lee Ann's instruction, he would have known that it was Reidel's night off and that Algeri was working at the club that night.

There was still the question of why Lee Ann would want her husband dead. The prosecution had a simple answer for this – money. They claimed that Lee Ann wanted Paul Reidel out of the picture so that she could start a new life with Salierno whilst living comfortably on Reidel's savings.

The prosecution, Denise Merrifield, believed that Lee Ann already started developing the plan to murder Reidel the first time she was in Florida in July 2000. Merrifield suggested that Lee Ann knew that if the husband and wife remained separated when Reidel was killed, she would be a number one suspect. Merrifield said that Lee Ann then pretended to reconcile with Reidel and moved back to New York, all whilst plotting his murder with Salierno. Her plan was to act like the grieving widow after his death, in order to seem innocent. As Reidel's wife, his fortune would be left to her and she would let some time pass before quietly moving back to Florida to be with Salierno.

Of course, the defence disputed this story. Defence attorney Bruce Barket maintained that Salierno went to New York in a fit of rage upon seeing that Lee Ann and Reidel were back together. Barket stated that Salierno's actions were irrational and not well planned; this is how he ended up shooting the wrong person. According to the defence, Lee Ann was oblivious to the fact that Salierno had killed Algeri and that her only wrong doing was the ongoing affair with Salierno.

In the end, it seemed like the decision could go either way for Lee Ann.

The Decision

The jury deciding the fate of Salierno returned to the court room in just four hours. He was found guilty of first degree murder and Judge Louis Ohlig sentenced him to life in prison with no parole.

Lee Ann's jury took longer to reach a decision. Her defence attorney believed that this was a good sign for her case. However, after four long days, the jury found her guilty too. Lee Ann was held equally responsible for the death of Alex Algeri. On the 28th April 2004, she was sentenced to twenty five years to life. The prosecution did not ask for life without parole for Lee Ann. They did not give any comment on why this was, which was unusual because the judge even stated that he would have happily given a longer sentence to Lee Ann had the prosecution asked for it.

Prosecutor Merrifield told the judge that "Justice has been served here, your honour. She, because of her own greed and evil heart, wanted her husband dead. This defendant is the most self-absorbed defendant I have ever prosecuted."

Bruce Barket, Lee Ann's defence attorney, was very upset by the outcome of the case. This is clear from his response to the decision: "I respect the Jury system. I respect the Jury process. I strongly disagree with the verdict."

Although Lee Ann's attorney claims to respect the Jury process, there has been some criticism of the way the case was handled in court. Some believe that the fact that Lee Ann and Salierno were tried in the same room was actually damaging to Lee Ann's case. The psychology of seeing the pair together, with the knowledge that they had an ongoing affair and a child together, could have affected the Jury's decision. The idea that Lee Ann was guilty of something was already in the minds of the Jury members, perhaps they found it hard to make an objective decision on Lee Ann's guilt in relation to the murder itself.

There was also the fact that the unintended victim of the murder was someone completely innocent and well liked. This caused wide spread anger, even those who did not know Alex Algeri felt that it was a real tragedy and an injustice. People were calling for the death penalty, though this was not requested by the prosecution. The high levels of emotion and anger surrounding the case could also have impacted on the Jury's decision making. It's hard to say if the reaction would have been the same if Reidel had been the one killed. It is possible that it would have been easier for the defence to portray Reidel as someone involved in a criminal lifestyle and Lee Ann as a fearful wife, desperate to escape his control. As Algeri was the victim, the Judge potentially felt a lot of pressure to dish out harsh sentences in an attempt to restore justice.

Alex Algeri was only 32 when he was murdered. His sister, Christie Stoll, told the judge "our brother is gone and the hole in our hearts will never be filled because of [Lee Ann's] greed and hatred of her husband. Even though Lee Ann Reidel wasn't there on the night of January 17th 2001, she just as well might have been. Lee Ann Reidel is just as guilty as Ralph Salierno." After the trial Algeri's father, Salvatore Algeri, said that "justice has been served completely."

Despite the defence claiming no evidence, and the issue raised about the nature of the trial, the widely held opinion is that justice was done and that Lee Ann was guilty for her part in Alex Algeri's murder.

Zachary, Lee Ann's third child, fathered by Salierno, is living with Lee Ann's sister in Long Island. Lee Ann and Reidel's son Nicholas is living with Reidel and no longer has any contact with his mother. Paul Reidel gave an insightful interview on the extremely popular talk show, Larry King live. He said that Lee Ann wanted him dead because she knew he would never stop fighting for access to their son. When asked if he felt lucky to have avoided murder, Reidel said "I don't feel lucky, because I would have took that walk. I would have never asked him to do it, and whatever happened, that's a burden I'll always carry." Reidel explained that his life is in order and his ongoing focus is raising his son. "I feel like I have a severe obligation to be a good man and do the right thing by my son because I feel like I owe that to Alex". King also asked Reidel what his feelings were towards Lee Ann, Reidel said that he did not hate her, but that he was confused and that he felt that she deserved the prison sentence.

Salierno is currently serving his sentence at Attica Correctional Facility in New York. Lee Ann is at Bedford Hills Correctional Facility also in New York. So far, her attempts to appeal have been unsuccessful.

KILL HIM JILL

Sarah Thompson

For some, gambling is a special treat - a past-time for birthdays, anniversaries and celebrations. It can be a bonding experience that brings everyone together through either luck, or misfortune. For others, gambling becomes an addiction, where they are willing to lie, cheat and steal in order to get their fix. For the lucky few, gambling can become a lifestyle. This lifestyle is often fraught with drugs, danger, embezzlement, lies and fraud. Like many of the stories that have come before them, the story of Bill Gustafik and Jill Rockcastle is one that would make any big-screenwriter proud. When you put in all the ingredients of drugs, grand theft, a professional poker player, a murder and an attempt at suicide, you get something that sounds so surreal, no one could have lived through it.

The truth is, Jill Rockcastle did live through it - but her husband, tragically, did not. While one's heart may feel the instinctive pull to go out to Jill, the reality is much worse. The story of Bill and Jill is set in Las Vegas, where gambling, drugs and danger go hand-in-hand. In the early morning hours of April 13th in 2007, police received an anonymous tip about a dead body on the 23rd floor of a condominium building. This was only the beginning of a web that would slowly begin to unravel, and make it clear that the story of Jill Rockcastle is almost indistinguishable from the story of Bill Gustafik - you cannot tell one story without the other. They're inseparable, even after death.

Jill Rockcastle and Bill Gustafik seemed like a couple who couldn't be happier. Jill and Bill met not long after Bill had divorced his previous wife in 2000. He had also graduated from chiropractor's school - a long way off from his eventual calling as a professional poker player. Meanwhile, Jill worked in the mortgage business, refinancing people's homes for them. It made her enough money to be independent and happy. Bill and Jill met in the months following his divorce, and hit it off as friends quite well. They started as friends, and stayed this way for about two years. But their relationship started to grow and build quite quickly. They eventually got married in 2005, but their relationship was one of devotion and obsession long before that. It was built on lies, secrets, fraud, and a desire to become better and more fabulous than the lives that they were currently leading.

Their relationship worked because, by Jill's own words, they discovered that they were able to get whatever they wanted out of people. However, their reasons were far different. Jill was able to manipulate the people around her because of what she described as "a need to survive." On the other hand, Bill did what he did out of, what Jill described as, "a need to conquer." In stark contrast to Jill's desires, Bill wanted to to be the most superior and successful person to walk into a room.

Their driving desires were far different, but they worked together all the same. Two master manipulators joined together to form a power couple that would lead them both to their eventual ends. Despite his good life, Bill wanted more. He longed to be one of the richest, most powerful people in the room when he walked in, and Jill was able to help him get it. Jill's inheritance money and her job as a refinancing for mortgages allowed her to live the lavish lifestyle that her partner craved. Even in the beginning of their relationship, the two worked together to manipulate whatever system was set up against them.

The Bill and Jill began their partnership in crime not long after they got together. Bill was going through a custody evaluation with his ex-wife. Both Bill and his ex-wife had been in a custody battle over their nine year old daughter for some time, perhaps all the time that Bill and Jill had known one another. Bill's child support payments would have been $4,000 given to his wife - but Bill asked Jill to re-worked his income in the books so that it looked as if he was being paid less than he actually was. Jill had software that was used to prepare your own tax returns. She showed him that she could alter the returns, and that brought bill out of the rage that had consumed him over the possibility of giving his ex-wife four grand in child support. Jill's solution was a savior - together, Bill and Jill worked their magic to cut down Bill's earnings.

Or was it magic? Jill's life story with Bill was left behind in a ten-page suicide note. While Jill Rockcastle never managed to go through with the planned attempt, the note leaves behind sordid and intimate details of their lives. The beginning of their schemes apparently started with a threat. In her note, Jill describes the first arrangement together, shedding more light on the custody scheme. At first, Jill refused Bill's request to arrange his income so that it looked as if he were earning less than he actually was. But then, Bill began to threaten her. A few days before the court hearing, Jill held the phone against her ear, listening to Bill bellow at her from the other end - screaming about how badly he needed her to do this for him. Like many women in her position, the threats and shouting worked, and Jill conceded to the plan.

And that plan also worked. The morning of the court hearing, Jill gave in and fixed the tax return documents to reflect a much lower income that Bill was truly earning. Their first scheme allowed for Bill to pay only $1,800 in child support - less than half of the proposed amount. In her 10 page letter, Jill wrote, "We began living without rules and not afraid of consequence." After all, what an exhilarating moment - to break the law and get away with it. It's no wonder that Jill and Bill became addicted to the thrill of it all. Not to mention, the money that came rolling in with it.

Bill Gustafik eventually opened up his own office in Antioch. Jill worked there with him, though her job behind the scenes was a bit different. She fixed the books in order to subtly increase the profit made between them. Jill was also instructed by Bill to finance real estate deals for some of the patients that came into Bill's chiropractor's office, in order for the income to go directly to Jill. The money that they made together was more than enough - and at the same time, it was nowhere near enough.

While Bill had his own talents when it came to these schemes, it was Jill who was the mastermind. In 2004, Bill took over one of this offices in Hayward, becoming the owner. Jill was the one who helped him purchase the entire building, and Jill was the one who helped him buy the building as an LLC, so that the purchase would have no effect on his personal credit. Meanwhile, Bill used his own talents in scamming his patients. Person after person, Bill would overcharge and over treat his patients in order to get as much money as possible. While Bill was doing this, it was Jill who was working behind the scenes for him - fixing his books, making sure that Bill was getting even more money than he worked for.

Jill had her own schemes, too. Independent of Bill, Jill Rockcastle worked deals, financing larger homes with large mortgages. On each home, Jill would get 2% or more on each one - that meant on a deal that was $700,000, Jill would take home $14,000. This allowed Jill to work less than Bill. In fact, she only worked once or twice a month. Even $8,000 was more than Jill usually spent in a month. While she was content with their level of riches, Bill wasn't. He wanted more, and with Jill at his side, he was determined to get it.

Bill wanted more of of life - even more than his 7 am to 7 pm lifestyle of scamming patients and fixed books was giving him. Bill began to obsess over getting on television. He wanted to play poker, and he wanted to do so on TV. Despite his already lavish lifestyle, Bill wanted more than just that. He wanted global recognition. Jill went along with it - after all, she had the time, and she has the devotion to Bill.

The note that had been left behind, written in Jill's own words, describes how it was around this time that the two of them went off to Las Vegas together - a city full of glittery lights, casinos, gambling, and eventual devastation. It was in October of 2004 that Jill followed Bill to Las Vegas. As she puts it, their move to Las Vegas was "the beginning of the con." Bill began to live the lifestyle that he believed he deserved - one that was lavish, with extravagant spending. It was Jill who continued to make it all possible, and Jill who continued to watch on. She helped him buy two houses, and get his extravagant car. Everything that Bill had and wanted was because of Jill. Without Jill Rockcastle, he would still be stuck, paying the $4,000 of child support to his ex wife. Bill's desire to be rich in a visible way left Jill vying to make herself worthy of him - she got plastic surgery, enhancing herself to look just like another one of Bill Gustafik glittering trophies.

Jill Rockcastle's letter reveals an even darker side of Bill - one that she, alone, was privy to. There was a time, undisclosed by the note, simply "two years ago", when Jill and Bill had Bill's daughter with them during Christmas time. Jill exposes the man Bill had been. All the time that they had been together, Jill had helped fix everything so that Bill would not have to pay the proposed amount to his ex-wife for child support. Despite Jill's abilities, Bill still wanted to problem gone once and for all. Jill described, in a note to Bill's ex wife, in a chilling lack of detail, that Bill had attempted to have his ex-wife and his ex mother in law killed.

An attempted assassination that didn't go through - the man had taken the money and bolted, leaving Bill both without his money, and Jill with the lasting impression of the lengths that Bill would go to. In Jill's note, she described she believed the Bill felt no love. In her note,

Jill says, "He knew deep down that he could not care for someone. [...] he didn't feel love. [...] he didn't feel compassion." This was the man that Jill had been living with for so long. If this man would attempt to put a hit out on his ex wife, there's no telling what he would do to Jill if she didn't continue to fund the lifestyle to which Bill was becoming accustomed.

Jill Rockcastle and Bill Gustafik were living a life that Jill's note described as "the life of fake millionaires". In Las Vegas, Bill finally began to play poker just as he had been obsessing over. The problem arose that Bill wasn't very good. In fact, his first night playing saw that Bill lost nearly ten thousand dollars. Their life together in Las Vegas wasn't everything that it seemed. The money was running out. Together, they were going broke. Their schemes continued on, the con growing and growing, until neither of them had complete control over what they were doing. The new schemes began with getting people to give Jill money. After all, Bill was still struggling with his ex-wife's custody battle. If he obtained more money, it would be scrutinized for child support. So it was Jill who ran the scams, and Jill who brought in the money.

The newest scam to get money was selling fake real estate. Jill allowed the cognitive dissonance get the better of her. Even some of the people who were supposedly their friends fell victim to Bill and Jill - there was nothing and no one that they couldn't con when they put their heads together. All the while, Jill told herself that she was helping out. Even if what they were doing was wrong, Jill was devoted to Bill. She loved him, and she wanted to help him. How could she say no? After all, they had left their lives behind, left behind Bill's doctor's offices, all for the bright light and excitements of Las Vegas. Bill wanted to be a high roller, and for a short while, Jill was rich. She allowed herself to block out the things that they were doing. In her letter, she says, "That's how I lived with my sick self."

But Bill was spending money faster than Jill could bring it it. He began to do drugs, and Jill would watch, dispassionate, as Bill would do lines of cocaine and play online poker. They were running out of money faster than Jill could replenish it. He would play a poker tournament and lose upwards of $15,000. Jill was a gambler as well, but she was better at it than Bill. She wasn't a poker player - rather her game of choice was Roulette. Jill could easily win thousands upon thousands of dollars. But, as quickly as Jill won $20,000 at Roulette, Bill would take it again. She would barely have time to text him of her winnings before he would come from the poker room, take it, and lose it again.

Jill began to squirrel money away. She knew that there was no possible way that they could keep going on like this. She kept money hidden from Bill, giving it to her children - both grown, at the time - if they ever needed it. Bill was beginning to get frustrated and desperate. Jill tucked away her money, and pulled several more scams that kept Bill in earnings to spend and lose. It was Jill who went to the bank to deposit money in order to keep their bills paid while Bill continued hemorrhage winnings. It was always Jill who had to deposit the money. Every once in awhile, Bill would give her cash and have her deposit it in the bank. The money had to look as if it were coming from Jill, least Bill's ex-wife become aware that Bill was skimming on his custody payments.

Jill was starting to breakdown. Her life had been reduced to running scams, telling lies, and bowing to Bill's whims. Jill knew that she had to stop Bill somehow. In her ten page suicide note, Jill describes, "I"m going to skip so many things in an effort to shorten this but my life was a constant hell for the last year. I'm going to skip all the lawsuits [...] All the tax notices. All the bounced checks. All the drugs." It was this hell that drove Jill to feeling as if she was the only one who was able to put a stop to Bill. She made phone calls to friends and other connections, feeling an ever overwhelming desperation. Jill even made a call to her attorney, desperate for someone to help her and get her out of the situation - her attorney only told her that Bill was addicted to gambling, and that the only thing to do is to wait until he has nothing left. But waiting was not something that Jill could, or would, do.

Jill took it into her own hands to stop bill, after having gone to the doctor and found out that the stress of the situation has started to give her shingles. At 7:30 in the evening, police received a call from an anonymous person, telling them of a dead body. When police investigators arrived, they wound Bill Gustafik dead. His body was in the master bedroom, and a kitchen knife was stashed away in the trash bin. The police had very little contention among them about who the suspect could be. Upon first glancing at the scene of the crime, they immediately suspected Jill Rockcastle.

The crime was quick. For Jill Rockcastle, killing her husband was not a drawn out plan, with weeks in the making. Nor was Bill Gustafik's death one that caused the police to go on a chase for their suspect. The night before what Jill called "the incident", the couple got into an argument - like most of the arguments in these days, it was about money. The day previous, Bill was leaving for the Bellagio Hotel, located in Las Vegas. He wanted Jill to pay his buy-ins for a poker tournament, and he wanted her to bring $30,000 for him to use. But Jill didn't bring the money. Either she couldn't get it, or she refused to. When she got to their shared Las Vegas condo, the couple began to argue. But the fight didn't end there. After going to sleep angry, Bill and Jill awoke in the morning to continue the same argument. Bill continued to demand Jill to give him money that he could play with. This time, Bill demanded $7,500 from her. Still, she refused.

Bill's aggression began to build. Jill's fears were starting to become realized. He was threatening to kill her, along with her ex wife. It was then that Jill made an attempt to leave. As she went to leave, Bill physically blocked her with his body. He forced her back from the door and into the kitchen. Jill grabbed a knife from the kitchen to defend herself, fearing for her life. The note described how Jill was afraid that

Bill would kill her, just as he had said that he would do. She couldn't escape him, though. He simply kept coming for her, and Jill did what she knew would stop Bill once and for all. She swing the knife into his chest, holding the weapon with both hands. When he went down, Jill still had the knife in her hands. In her own words, Jill says she "just snapped".

Jill stabbed him over fifteen times. Just like that, Bill was gone. There was no grand plan. After years of scamming, scheming, lying and cheating, Jill was done. The story of Bill and Jill ends the way so many women's stories have ended - a dead husband, a knife in their hands, years of fear and abuse behind them. While the story leading up to Bill's death involved so many lies, and so many cons, the story of his death is an anticlimactic one. A death that Bill wouldn't have been proud of - the only thing that made him notable in death was the same that made him notable in life: his wife, Jill. And though Bill had gone out as many men do, stabbed and left for dead, it was Jill Rockcastle that made sure everyone would remember his name, and her own.

After he was dead, Jill cleaned up after herself, cleaned herself up, and fled from the condo. Just like that, Bill Gustafik was dead and Jill Rockcastle was on the run. She had stopped him, just as she knew that she had to do. It was then that Jill Rockcastle disappeared, and on the Monday after Bill Gustafik's death, Jill Rockcastle sent an email to her friends, family and various business partners. The email included ten pages of a suicide note. The note goes in depth on all of Jill's struggles throughout her time of having known Bill, and all of the things that had happened to her. The note describes Bill's struggles with his gambling addiction, and many of the scams and schemes that they had performed today. It was, essentially, ten pages of confessions, implicating herself in all of the things that she and Bill had done together. But, it was always a note to tell everyone goodbye.

In her email, Jill wrote: "This is my final statement done to help all the people affected by my actions [...] and the results of whatever happen to them in our aftermath. I'm writing this so that each person that receives it will identify with the time period in which your experience occurred with him and I and can have some of the why [...] answered. I am not trying in anyway to justify a single thing in here. I am not looking to clear my name or actions. I have already done the most final things possible to stop us from hurting anyone else."

The email was a suicide note, one that was meant to tell everyone that nothing that she and Bill had done would ever touch them again. She alludes here to Bill's death, and to what she had planned to do in order to "stop us" from continuing on how she had been.

Of course, police investigators couldn't let Jill Rockcastle get away with what she had done by allowing her to kill herself. An attempt to find Jill where she had fled was made, first by searching her home in San Ramon that she had kept with Bill. The Las Vegas police called the San Ramon police and urged them to go to the home that Jill and Bill had owned together in San Ramon, in order to arrest her or take her to the hospital, depending on how far she had gone through with her plan to end her life.

However, police investigators were shocked to find that Jill Rockcastle was not in her home in San Ramon. When the police broke down her door, there was no one. Another anonymous call was given to the Las Vegas police, this time urging them on to another location, this time in San Luis Obispo. The call advised them that Jill could be found at a bed and breakfast by the name of Petit Soleil Bed and Breakfast. The San Luis Obispo police searched the small establishment, and found her in her room. She was unconscious, having attempted to end her life with an overdose , just as she had stated that she would in her email.

It was three days after the initial murder when Jill Rockcastle was finally found and apprehended. After the email had gone out, people had begun coming forward with stories of their experiences with Jill Rockcastle and Bill Gustafik. Some people were adamant that Bill didn't deserve what he had got, even if he was a scammer and a cheat. Many people also described Jill has being aggressive herself, with a cocaine habit that matched her husband's. More and more people came forward to tell their stories about how the couple had cheated them out of property and money.

It was Jill's email that had described Bill as aggressive and dangerous, detailing all of the ways in which she was afraid of him. As more people came out of the woodwork as victim's of Jill and Bill, a new light was beginning to be shed on Jill herself. Jim Rivera, one of Bill Gustafik's closest friends from when they were younger, described the Bill in Jill's letter as "inconsistent" with the man that he had known his whole life. Another anonymous friend, this one of Rockcastle, described Jill has being the one to lure Bill into a relationship. Jill was the mastermind, people who knew the couple said. In court, attorneys said that Jill Rockcastle showed no signs of battered woman's syndrome, as both her own public defender and ten page email tried to claim.

Perhaps no one will ever know the truth of what happened between Bill Gustafik and Jill Rockcastle. All that is known is the memories of the couple, the memories of Bill, and the email that had been sent to friends, family and business contacts. Jill had intended to be dead after sending that email, so there is no telling what is truth, exaggeration, or fiction, when Jill did not expect to have to answer for her crime, or the story that she left behind.

BLACK WIDOW KRISTIN ROSSUM

AIMEE BAXTER

Photos of a beautiful, lively little girl, her blonde hair in pigtails as she dances The Nutcracker in her little pink tutu. That same adorable child laughingly enjoying holidays with her family at their home. These are the pictures that Constance Rossum will show you of her daughter Kristin.

Bright, vivacious, and uncommonly beautiful are the words used to describe Kristin Rossum as a child. The child that everyone said was so smart and pretty, the one who modeled for department stores and who excelled in her schoolwork, the one with what seemed to be the perfect suburban childhood.

However, as many already know ... looks can be deceiving.

Idyllic Child becomes a Rebellious Teen

Born to Ralph and Constance Rossum on October 25, 1976, in Claremont, California, Kristin Rossum wanted for nothing. Kristin was the first child of Ralph Rossum – a professor at Claremont McKenna College – and his wife Constance – who worked at Azusa Pacific University. Even when her first and then second little brother was born, Kristin remained her parent's sweet little princess.

When Ralph accepted a position as President of Hampden-Sydney College in southern Virginia, the family moved across the country from California to Virginia. It was 1991 and Kristin was a delicate 15 years old. Her parents enrolled her in an all-girl boarding school in Richmond, Virginia named St. Catherine's School.

That seems to be the beginning of the end of Kristin's innocence. At the private school, Kristin made friends quickly and soon was very popular. She became the party girl smoking, drinking, and using marijuana liberally.

In 1992, at just 16 years old, Kristin is introduced to methamphetamines – a strong Central Nervous System (CNS) stimulant – and is soon hooked. Within a few weeks, she was using Crystal Meth (also known as Crank, Speed, Chalk, etc.) daily. She was a tweaker (slang used to describe a methamphetamine addict).

Kristin the Druggie

When asked about it later, Kristin recalled her first time using meth by saying "I remember it feeling good, a kind of euphoria. You feel very revved up and energetic and happy. I wanted to feel that all the time."

Soon, Kristin's straight As were slipping to become Cs and Ds. She lost weight rapidly and began to withdraw from her family and any friends who were not using meth. According to later court records, Kristin is described as having "an almost insatiable need for crystal meth."

It was not long before Kristin developed all the character traits that addicts hone to conceal and continue their freedom to use. Lying, manipulation, and theft became the new norm for young Kristin Rossum.

Her parents were understandably at a loss for how to deal with this behavior. After all, not that long ago they were tucking her into her pink canopy bed and kissing her goodnight with a song and a prayer. However, the lack of consequences established by her parents could be a contributing factor in her later misdeeds.

At first, they ignored their daughter's erratic and rapidly devolving character, chalking it up to teenage angst. Eventually, they could not turn a blind eye anymore and they soon realized that their daughter was not who they thought she was.

Later, both Ralph and Constance cite an incident in 1993 as the first time they admitted their daughter had a problem. After returning from a cruise in April of that year, the Rossums found that their sweet, perfect daughter had in fact stolen their credit cards, personal checks, and a video camera.

Confronted with the missing items, Kristin pointed to some of her friends (fellow druggies) as the thieves. They say that she admitted to using some of the cash to buy drugs but insisted that the rest was stolen by somebody else. Her parents accepted Kristin's excuse and did not report the theft to police.

According to Constance's testimony later, Kristin's erratic behavior came to a head in December of 1993. Ralph Rossum – convinced Kristin was still using drugs – attempted to search his daughter's backpack. She resisted, they struggled, and he struck her several times in the arm to get the bag away from her.

However, that was not the end of the incident. Sobbing and enraged, Kristin grabbed a knife from the kitchen and slashed at her wrists. When that did not work, she ran upstairs to the bathroom, locked herself inside, and began hacking at her wrists with a razor. Later Kristin told the court, "I felt devastated ... I didn't know how to deal with the situation ... I wanted them to see how sorry I was."

Her wounds, however, were superficial and her parents treated them at home. They later said that they were "afraid of what would happen if they took her to the hospital." They feared that if they told the hospital that she had cut herself, they would have committed her for a psychiatric evaluation and if they tested her blood and found drugs, they would report her to the police.

It is likely that the reason none of the cuts were serious was that Kristin did not intend them to be. Psychologists later speculated that it was merely a way for her to manipulate her parents. If it was, it worked.

Again, Kristin escaped any immediate consequences for her bad behavior. Again, her parents made excuses for her behavior and thus enable her to continue that behavior. Cryptically, one entry in her diary after this incident contained the morbidly, prophetic words, "I could get away with murder."

A few days after this incident, a teacher noticed the marks on Kristin (or she possibly showed them to her intentionally). She called the police to the school to investigate the possibility of child abuse.

Officer Larry Horowitz of the Claremont Police investigated and testified that Kristin told him that her father had hit her and that her mother had "called her a slut and said she was worthless." After interviewing Ralph and Constance Rossum, Officer Horowitz concluded that there had been no abuse and the case was closed.

In January 1994, Constance found a glass pipe hidden in Kristin's underwear drawer. She eventually called Officer Horowitz and Kristin was handcuffed, arrested, and held for several hours at Claremont Municipal Jail.

Kristin finally had her first taste of culpability. She seemed to clean her act up and after graduating, she enrolled part-time at the University of Redlands in California. However, soon she relapsed and dropped out of school without a word to her family and simply disappeared. She moved to Chula Vista – a suburb of San Diego near the Mexican border.

A Chance Encounter

After a month of hard partying, drinking, smoking meth, and hiding from her parents, Kristin was walking the pedestrian bridge that led from Chula Vista to Tijuana, Mexico. Authorities speculate that at the time she was likely on her way to meet her supplier in Mexico on that fateful day.

As she crossed the bridge, Kristin Rossum dropped her jacket. Before she could retrieve it, a handsome young man that she later described as reminding her of John Stamos, had picked it up and was handing it to her. It was Greg de Villers and he later told friends "it was love at first sight." They chatted in French while Greg's younger brother paced nearby.

She returned to the Southern California apartment where de Villers lived with his brothers, Bertrand and Jerome, and a friend, Christopher Wren. She never left.

Within a few weeks, the couple was professing their love and de Villers had sworn to help Kristin kick her meth addiction. Greg's brothers and Wren were not happy and prompted him to end the relationship. They had noticed that things were coming up missing from the apartment since Kristin's arrival and knew of her drug problem.

According to a statement given later by de Villers' friend and roommate Christopher Wren, Kristin had told him that she felt like being with Greg was the wrong choice. For some reason, Wren chose not to tell his buddy.

Even if Wren had told de Villers about Kristin's doubts, it is unlikely that it would have made any difference. Greg de Villers was adamant, he loved Kristin Rossum no matter what her faults and he was going to save her from herself.

By May of 1995, it looked as though he had done just that. By all accounts, it looked like Kristin was clean and free of the hold meth had on her. She reestablished contact with her worried parents and it looked like Kristin was finally moving towards the bright future her parents had envisioned for their little girl.

The Rossums looked at Greg de Villers as if he was an angel for all that he had done for Kristin. Constance Rossum, in an interview with the CBS news magazine "48 Hours," put it like this, "We always called Greg our godsend from heaven. I mean, of all the people she could have met, to have met a nice, decent person who wanted to take care of her, we thanked God."

Soon, Kristin enrolled at San Diego State University. Her professors later said described Rossum as a stellar student with one going so far as to describe her as "among the most promising students" he had "ever taught."

Everyone who knew her believed she was happy. She was earning straight As and in 1998, she graduated cum laude (with honors). She got a job at San Diego Medical Examiner's office as a toxicologist.

Constance would later testify, "Our old Kristin was back," and she thanked God and de Villers – in that order – for the change.

Storybook Love?

Everyone who knew them described Kristin and Greg as the perfect couple. Constance Rossum testified later that when they were together they were "like a couple of lovebirds." When they announced their engagement, nobody was surprised.

However, as is often the case, outward appearances did not accurately represent reality. There was a layer of tension beneath the surface of de Villers and Rossum's storybook love affair. Kristin's closest friends knew that she had a hard time staying faithful and monogamous.

According to prosecutor's later, Kristin actually maintained a "graphically flirtatious" correspondence with a former boyfriend and at least one other man during at least some portion of her relationship with de Villers. Rossum even went to her mother only a month before she was supposed to walk down the aisle and broke down in tears as she told her mother that she wanted to cancel the wedding.

Constance Rossum considered her daughter's outburst to be cold feet, pre-wedding jitters that would pass. After all, Greg de Villers was the man who led her out of the darkness of addiction and Constance could not see how Kristin could possibly want to end the relationship.

She would soon tell the court, "I gave her the wrong counsel, I'm afraid."

The wedding was spectacular. The video shows a smiling and laughing Kristin Rossum, now Kristin de Villers, dancing with her new husband and looking happy. As for de Villers, he is recorded on that video saying, "Kristin is the most wonderful person I've ever met. I just can't wait to spend the rest of my life with her."

Only seven months after the wedding, however, Kristin Rossum told her mother that she felt "trapped like a bird in a cage." It was January 2000 and Kristin's journal shows that she had begun souring on her marriage only a couple of months after the wedding.

Greg de Villers did not show any sign that he felt the same or even knew of his wife's misgivings and doubt. Conversely, his brother Jerome later testified that Greg was ecstatically happy and never spoke of anything even smacking of marital discord. Even his colleagues at a genetics research firm where de Villers worked, described him as happily married and devoted to his wife. Some even went so far as to describe Greg de Villers as "sickeningly in love with his wife."

Friends of Greg de Villers said that he was often talking about his plans for their future together. He bragged about his wife's accomplishments, both big and small, and often spoke of starting a family. One friend remembers him saying that he wanted "all girls who were as beautiful and smart as Kristin."

At the same time, his adored wife was painting a much grimmer portrait of her marriage and her husband. She often complained to colleagues and friends about Greg, saying that he was moody, controlling, and domineering. Later, in an interview with "48 Hours," Kristin said, "Greg became very, very clinging... I tried to pull away and have some sort of independence."

An email sent to her brother Brent only 11 months after the wedding showed how she truly felt. She wrote, "I should have trusted my own instincts and called off the wedding. Now I'm stuck with the heavy realization that I married the wrong person."

A New Love Affair

Not long after Kristin Rossum sent that email to her brother, she met Dr. Michael Robertson. Newly hired as Chief Toxicologist at the San Diego Medical Examiner's office, Robertson was Kristin's immediate supervisor and she began spending large amounts of time with him.

Soon, they were spending time together outside of work. Kristin found danger and excitement in her passionate affair with her handsome, Australian doctor – who was also married. Her husband – and the problems she seemed to have with him – disappeared from Kristin's consideration and soon she was talking with friends outside of her colleagues about the wonderful new man in her life who she described as "a big hunk of an Australian guy."

By early May, Rossum was receiving inappropriate emails and notes from her boss. A search of her desk later turned up love notes and IOUs for things such as "a night of lovemaking" from Robertson. Coworkers later reported that Robertson was often seen sauntering into work with a bouquet of flowers that would soon end up on Rossum's desk.

In June, according to court records, Kristin Rossum had given her lover a gift. A book titled "52 Invitations To Great Sex" she had inscribed on the inside cover, "Well, sweetheart, together we'll enjoy a lifetime of passion."

When asked later, Rossum said, "I felt like I was in love. It was very romantic, very exciting, very passionate."

In August of 2000, Kristin turned to her best friend, Melissa Prager. Prager later told the court that he friend confided in her that she was madly in love with Robertson but was "terrified" by the idea of telling Greg she wanted a divorce.

In October 2000, Greg de Villers was still telling his friends, family, co-workers, and anyone else who would listen about his love for his wife and his plans for their future. His brother Jerome later told the court that around Halloween, Greg was talking about his excitement over taking his future children with Kristin out to trick or treat.

However, Kristin Rossum had reached a conclusion about her marriage. She told her close friends that she was looking for an apartment and planned to leave her husband.

'Til Death Do Us Part

It is unclear how de Villers learned of his wife's infidelity and plan to leave him. Rossum has always claimed that she told Greg de Villers about the affair and that her admission launched a spiraling depression in her husband.

According to Kristin Rossum, she told her husband about Robertson and he demanded the man's phone number. When Kristin supplied the number (although why she would is uncertain), de Villers called her boss and lover and demanded that he break off their relationship.

There is no court record of a response to this demand by Robertson. However, the relationship continued.

Authorities, however, have a very different set of circumstances in mind for how Greg discovered Kristin's infidelity.

They maintain that de Villers found out about the affair on accident in the fall of 2000. This was after Kristin and Robertson were sent to Milwaukee together to attend a toxicology conference. According to court records, despite being booked into separate hotels – likely due to rumors in the office about their relationship – the duo rented their own room together and spent several nights from September 30 to October 7 together in that room.

A coworker saw Kristin at the conference during the week and noted that she was no longer wearing her wedding ring.

One of the conferences that Rossum and Robertson attended in Milwaukee was on the deadly effects of fentanyl. Fentanyl is a clear, odorless narcotic that is 100 times stronger than morphine. It is generally administered to cancer patients whose pain is not eased by other means. It is so potent that it only takes a few drops to kill.

The seminar also discussed the fact that the drug is so rarely prescribed and used that most medical examiner's offices do not test for it. Both Rossum and Robertson were well aware of the fact that their office did not test for fentanyl.

During the three years that Rossum had worked in the San Diego Medical Examiner's office, only seven cases of death by overdose had involved fentanyl. She had seen 15 patches and 1 vial of the drug in a powder form. It was Rossum's job to log and track the drugs in her logbook. It was Robertson's job to hold the key to the cabinet those substances was then stored in.

These were facts that seemed innocuous at the time but would soon hold a more serious meaning.

Returning to Old Ways

Only a day or two after returning from Milwaukee, Rossum sent de Villers an email telling him that she was taking three different prescription drugs "to help with the severe anxiety I've been experiencing as a result of our relationship. You've hurt me beyond repair."

Not only was Kristin taking prescription medications, she had fallen back into her addiction to meth. After some of the drugs went missing from her office, Robertson admitted later that he found traces of the drug in her desk and rather than turning his girlfriend in, he flushed the drugs down the toilet. Then he covered for her with his superiors.

Once again, Kristin Rossum has done something bad. Once again, somebody shields her from the ramifications of her actions. Once again, there are no consequences for Kristin's bad actions.

Severing Ties

By early November 2000, Rossum was ready to end her relationship with de Villers. She insisted she wanted only a "trial separation."

She later told detectives that de Villers literally collapsed when she told him she was leaving him. She claimed that he lay in bed for days afterward and would not communicate with her. She later told the court, "It was painful for me, too, to see someone you love hurt so much." She still never owned up to the fact that it was her own actions that caused her husband that pain.

On November 6, 2000, just after 9:15 pm, Kristin Rossum called 991.

She claimed that her husband was unresponsive and that she was doing CPR to try and revive him. When paramedics arrived, however, they found Rossum on the phone in the living room. Her husband was lying lifeless on their bed.

Gregory de Villers lay dead in his La Jolla bedroom with rose petals covering his chest. Besides his lifeless head lay a copy of his wedding picture ... less than two years old. Nearby on the floor lay a crumpled love letter from the dashing Australian doctor that was his wife's boss and lover. Beside that was his wife's discarded diary, open to an entry that she had left confiding that she felt her marriage was the biggest mistake of her life.

For all intents and purposes, it looked like a suicide. His distraught widow claimed that Greg had learned that her affair with Robertson was still happening.

However, de Villers' brother Jerome adamantly refused to accept that his brother had committed suicide. The entire de Villers family demanded an investigation. Still, the San Diego police were hesitant to open an investigation.

The Truth and Nothing but the Truth

Their opinion quickly changed and authorities soon came to suspect Kristin Rossum, de Villers' 26-year-old blonde beauty of a wife. They believed that she had used her knowledge as a toxicologist and the information that she had gleaned from working in the medical examiner's office to poison her husband.

Due to concerns over a conflict of interest, de Villers' autopsy was outsourced to another lab in Los Angeles. That lab is one of the few in the country that tests for fentanyl. They found 7 times the lethal dose of fentanyl in de Villers' system.

Two weeks after de Villers' death, the San Diego police brought Kristin Rossum in for interrogation. She reiterated to police that her husband had been extremely depressed.

According to Kristin Rossum's story, on the Thursday before de Villers' death, they struggled over a letter that she had sticking out of her back pocket. In her account, de Villers' attempted to grab the letter from her pocket and knocked her to the ground to wrest it from her. She claimed that it was the first time she had been afraid of her husband.

When he had the letter, as Rossum's story goes, he held it out and threatened to take it to his wife's office and expose the affair as well as her reoccurring meth addiction. She took the letter and shredded it but de Villers pieced it back together.

In court, Rossum's parents described the night, two days before de Villers' death, when they went over to visit the couple for dinner. Ralph Rossum testified that de Villers seemed to be deeply depressed, "a man spiraling down."

Kristin Rossum's father continued to describe how de Villers had drunk heavily that night. He drank wine and gin until his father in law had to tell him to lower his voice. Constance Rossum described

Greg de Villers' voice as "fraught with melodrama" as he spoke at length about the dozen red roses that he had given to Kristin for her birthday a few days earlier.

She testified that he seemed depressed, agitated, and particularly obsessed with the fact that all but one had died and shed its petals. In a TV interview, she gave months after the death, Rossum stated, "He was making a big deal of the last rose standing. I think he was just making a statement that he knew our relationship was over."

Things rapidly spiraled from that point on. Police learned that Rossum had relapsed and was using meth again.

On June 25, 2001 – 7 months after Greg de Villers' death – his wife was arrested on charges of First Degree Murder. She spent over six months in jail and then on January 4, 2002, her parents posted $1.25 million for bail.

During the trial, the prosecution contended that she killed her husband to keep him from telling her bosses that she was having an affair with Robertson and that she was stealing meth from the office. They presented evidence that she had the knowledge about fentanyl to use it, access to the drug (remember the missing fentanyl from her office), and the motive to kill her husband.

On November 12, 2002, Kristin Rossum was found guilty of first-degree murder.

Exactly one month later on December 12, she was sentenced to life in prison without the chance of parole. She was transferred from the San Diego jail to the Central California Women's Facility in Chowchilla California – the largest women's correctional facility in the United States.

Distant Repercussions

In 2006, the de Villers family filed a lawsuit against Rossum and San Diego County for wrongful death. They were asking for $50 million but on March 25, 2006, a San Diego jury ordered Rossum to pay more than $100 million in punitive damages to the de Villers family. The same judge ordered San Diego County to pay $1.5 million.

According to the de Villers' lawyer John Gomez, the punitive damages awarded in this case are the most assessed against an individual defendant in California history. The jury apparently awarded double what the de Villers' family was asking for due to the estimation that Rossum could make $60 million from selling the rights to her story.

The judge later lowered the awarded amounts to $10 million in punitive damages and $4.5 million in a compensatory award.

In September of 2010, a 3-judge panel of the 9th US Circuit Court of Appeals ruled that Rossum's lawyers should have challenged the prosecutions assertion that she poisoned her husband with fentanyl by demanding their own tests. Due to this, the panel ordered a San Diego federal court to hold a hearing into whether the defense's error could have affected the trial's outcome.

On September 13, 2011, the US Court of Appeals withdrew its opinion and replaced it with a one-paragraph statement that denied Rossum's petition.

Conclusion

Kristin Rossum will spend the rest of her life behind bars. She has exhausted her state appeals and the federal courts denied her petition to be heard.

Her contention remains that her husband killed himself. She further believes that he did it the way that he did to point the finger of guilt at her. She vehemently insists that she did not kill her husband.

At one point, Kristin Rossum even suggested that her lover the handsome Australian doctor might have killed her husband. He knew about de Villers' threat to expose them before his death and had access to the fentanyl.

For his part, Robertson returned to Brisbane, Australia only one month after de Villers' death under the excuse that he had to care for his ailing mother. In September of 2013, the San Diego Reader reported that prosecutors filed a criminal complaint against Robertson in 2006 charging him with one count of conspiracy to obstruct justice.

If he returned to the US, Robertson could face up to three years in prison. In 2001, Robertson was named as an "unindicted co-conspirator" in Rossum's trial.

As of 2014, Robertson was running a forensic consulting business in Brisbane.

Kristin Rossum, the sweet spoiled only daughter of college professors, who was never held accountable for her actions as she grew up will spend the rest of her days within the walls of the largest women's correctional facility in the US. She is finally going to have to answer for what she has done.

GWEN HENDRICKS

Gwen Gillespie Hendricks was born into a Navy family in Memphis, Tennessee in 1955.

Her father was a naval officer while her mother was a housewife. Like most military families, they moved often from station to station, according to her father's assignment. Growing up in a devoutly Catholic home and Gwen would embrace the religion with fervor.

Gwen dressed with modesty, wearing button down shirts and minimal make-up. She fostered a nerd look, with wire-rimmed glasses and short hair.

Carrying on the family's military tradition, she joined the Air Force at the age of twenty-five. It was there she would meet Jim Hendricks, twenty-four, who was her instructor.

Jim Hendricks was a tall, strapping Air Force sergeant with an air of authority. He had an easy smile and Gwen found him easy on the eyes.

"Well, it was kind of instant attraction," Gwen recalled. "There was a bit of lust there as he's a very tall, handsome man. The Air Force can tell you that you can't date but they can't tell you who to marry so I went to the Jag office and asked if I could marry my STA and they said 'yes.'"

The two were married in 1980. Jim had a five year old daughter, Season Hendricks, from a previous relationship. In 1982, they would have a son, Ben.

Because of their career choice, the couple spent a lot of time apart during the early years of their marriage. Jim was stationed at Wake Island while Gwen was assigned to Eglin Air Force Base in Florida.

The couple would be reunited in 1986 as Jim was assigned to the Air Force Academy in Colorado Springs. Gwen would not re-enlist in the Air Force, instead taking a job with the Internal Revenue Service.

The couple spent three years in Colorado before Jim would be transferred to Guam in August of 1989. He took the the entire family with him to the island.

"I figured we had a pretty normal family," Season said. "Until we moved to Guam. Things started to change. She (Gwen) would pick fights. She was jealous of the time my Dad and I would spend together."

"She (Gwen) had a different life in mind for herself," forensic psychologist Joyce Smith said. "She was used to having her own money. So when they moved to Guam there was little to do and less money to do it with."

Gwen and the children moved back to the United States, returning to Colorado and leaving Jim in Guam.

She would buy a home in Littleton and once again start working for the IRS. She then joined the junior Chamber of Commerce where she met Terry Knaack and a woman named Rochelle.

"Rochelle was into tarot cards," Gwen said. "And Terry was into new age occultism. My religion, my faith was still very meaningful to me. I wanted to do Bible study with them to get them out of what I considered witchcraft. Rochelle said she wouldn't go to Bible study with me unless I did the cards with her and the same with Terry. So I think I opened up the door to hell. Right after I started, everything went wrong"

During this time, Gwen began to experience health issues. She suffered from dizzy spells and nausea.

Her personality shifted as well, changing from being even-tempered to easily agitated and manic. With her health and ability to focus effected, Gwen stepped down from her revenue collector position to tax examiner.

"Could the illness have played a part in her deciding to kill her husband?" Smith asked. "Maybe. But Gwen was really steeped into religion and sounded like she embraced some of the more fringe elements of Christianity. She truly believed that occultism was a form of witchcraft and that those things could do her harm. So when she suffered from her illness she erroneously attributed it to her dabbling in the occult. She was a woman who preferred supernatural explanations to rational thought."

Gwen also started to grow deeper into debt, buying expensive gifts for friends.

In the fall of 1990, Gwen hired Terry Knaack to help remodel the Littleton home. A few months later, Knaack moved into the couple's basement with the rationale being he would be able to help with the mortgage. With the husband away and a man in the home, Gwen began to fantasize about Terry and starting over with him.

"Terry would talk a lot about wanting to having a ranch for children with special needs," Gwen recalled. "And I started having delusions that he and I would start this ranch together for the children."

"She entered into a fantasy world," Smith said. "She began imagining a life with this other man, having delusions of grandeur of what they would do together. He became her willing accomplice in her dreams, since her own husband was absent because of military duty. So an alternate universe with Terry Knaack became her obsession. What probably started as harmless day dreams soon grew into something sinister."

"I also believe that Gwen had more than a little bit of a Messiah complex. She had this compulsion to save people and it manifested in doling out gifts and handouts to people who she felt were in need. She had this secret life and kept things from Jim who was away on military assignment. Those secrets involved getting into credit card debt."

By January of 1991, Gwen began telling friends that she was having premonitions of Jim dying in a plane crash.

"I had this really bad dream over and over again," Gwen recalled. "Where Jim had died in a plane crash. I was thinking, well after Jim died that I would marry Terry and we'd start this ranch but of course Terry didn't know anything about because it was all in my head."

Gwen then began hearing voices.

"They (the voices) wanted me to sacrifice what was most dear in my life," Gwen recalled. "I remember thinking that I have to answer these voices because this is coming from God. You know, I've got to sacrifice what I loved the most and that was Jim."

Gwen kept a journal where she logged the "premonitions" of her husband's death. She titled the journal "The Courage to Will and Persevere," She described the voices that she heard and believed that God had told her to kill Jim.

"She experienced what we call 'command hallucinations,'" said Smith. "These are sometimes coupled with someone's value system, in this case, it was Gwen's religion. Gwen believed that she should obey God and believed that the voices that she heard were, in fact, coming from God. So this could go bad real quick if those voices told her to do damage to someone."

"She was past the breaking point, a delusional schizophrenic that was not diagnosed. When she confided with friends it was probably with people who shared her same point of view, people who believed in visions, messages from God and premonitions. Gwen was a soft-spoken woman and even if someone thought she was crazy they would not think she would be capable of taking a gun and blowing someone's brains out. She didn't have that violent vibe."

But behind closed doors, Gwen would deal with problems or difficulties in a haphazard fashion. She would often open up the Bible and believed that whatever random verse she came upon was a direct message from God.

"I reread Psalm 90 quite a few times before a small voice said, 'Keep reading, keep reading.'" Gwen wrote in her journal. "After reading the first page of stanzas, I knew I would be protected from the car bombs, the knifings, the guns, the contracts and all the other evil I had seen connected with busting the pornographers and pimps. Those mafia guys play rough, but somehow they just won't be able to get me. Then I turned the page to continue reading. It felt like a giant fist had slammed into my heart. I literally could not breath [sic]. I burst into sobs and sunk to the floor. I cried for Jim because he really was going to die."

Gwen began to prepare for Jim's death, taking out a $300,000 life insurance policy on her husband payable on his death.

She then visited a local banker, informing him that she would be soon be receiving proceeds from insurance claim. Gwen was told that she would not be able to use the money as long as Jim was alive. She then forged a doctor's note which alleged that she had multiple sclerosis. She submitted this note to the Red Cross along with a letter stating that they should be responsible for being her husband back from Guam.

Gwen did not want the proceeds from the insurance for her own material gain. She believed that she could use the proceeds from his life insurance to establish the "James Hendricks Foundation" to aid victims of mafia produced pornography.

"She became obsessed with pornographers," Smith said. "Like most people with Messiah Complexes, she chose an ill of society and focused on that, believing that she was a chosen vessel to help eradicate the 'sin'. In her deluded mind, she needed this money to accommodate God's will to establish this ranch wherein she would save victims of pornography. The only way she could attain this goal would be to kill Jim and take the life insurance proceeds."

"I was very desperate to have him (Jim) back," Gwen said. "I felt like I was at my limit and not really realizing that I actually was really having a breakdown."

With her husband not even dead yet, Gwen began purchasing clothes for herself and the children to wear for his funeral.

She bought silk flowers and boxes of Kleenex for mourning friends and family.

Gwen also increased the amount of Jim's life insurance from $300,000 to $1,000,000.

True to her premonition, she bought a wedding dress for herself and put a wedding ring on layaway for Knaack.

Gwen would ask God to speak to her directly and "guide her hand" as she thumbed through her Bible. When she got to a passage, she would believe that was what God wanted her to study."

"For the first reading, only the last sentence made sense," Gwen wrote. "I had asked if what I felt about Jim's death was real. He said yes.

God can even speak through the dictionary!

After reading the first page of stanzas, I knew I would be protected from car bombs, the knifings, the guns, the contracts and all the other evil I had seen connected with busting pornographers and pimps. Those Mafia guys play rough, but somehow they just won't be able to get me."

"You can see her delusions of grandeur in her journal writings," Smith said. "She had all of the symptoms of a delusional narcissist, truly believing that God made her as the 'Chosen One.'"

Gwen would write that she had a two-way conversation with God about creating the ranch.

"'Oh, so the ranch is in Douglas county near to the Springs so my family will be protected from the mafia guys' Then I knew in Denver, I'm Gwen Hendricks. In the Springs, I'm Gwen Knaack. I had thought the clinic would carry the name of the ranch, but with this new insight, I knew that for safety sake, everything had to be kept separate."

She continued to have health issues as well, as the nausea and attacks of dizziness still had not subsided. Physicians could not determine the cause of her illness. She was eventually diagnosed with Ménière's disease, an ailment that causes vertigo and a fluctuating hearing loss. She had a micro-shunt placed into her ear which only helped relieve the pain she was experiencing.

Her mental health, however, continued to deteriorate.

Jim would return to Colorado for good in May of 1991. It would not be a well-received reunion, however, as the couple fought over everything specifically the living arrangements of Knaack. Jim promptly kicked the boarder out of the home.

He then took control of the finances as he discovered that Gwen had maxed out the credit cards.

"My brother said that she had apparently taken several other credit cards and had maxed them out to the limit," recalled Steve Hendricks, Jim's brother. "And he was furious with her at that point. He did confide in me that he was thinking about leaving Gwen."

Jim would take away all of Gwen's credit cards and this made her extremely angry.

"He took away her power," Smith said. "She got an ego boost by buying expensive gifts for friends and helping out women that she thought were in need. When Jim took that away, she saw him as someone who needed to be eliminated."

Divorce seemed imminent but Gwen seemed immune to it all in her journal writings.

"The funeral, the ranch school, children, the foundation, always being pushed forward," she wrote. *"I have to do what I have to do, too. But just for now I'm going to take one day at a time. I'm hoping I don't get too compulsed to do anything more for at least this coming week. I need to rest.*

Perhaps I should start by explaining the little voice. It's my voice, but not me. It comes from somewhere inside, and if I don't listen to it, act on it, it becomes a compulsion. If I don't listen and act on the compulsion, it grows stronger and stronger until it dominates all aspects of my life. I learned long ago to listen and do what I'm told. Things work out when I do, and when I don't, things get real miserable...Yes, my little voice is the way God reaches me with the Holy Spirit."

With Jim now home on a permanent basis, The voices in her head grew louder. They began to speak with more urgency in telling her that she had to kill her husband.

"True to her religious background, she did not interpret auditory hallucinations as a sign of mental illness," Smith said. "Gwen was the kind of woman who took the stories in the Bible literally, seeing herself as a modern day Abraham who heard voices from God. You hear it in the way she describes the voices in her head telling her to sacrifice her husband in the same way the Bible speaks of God telling Abraham to sacrifice his son Isaac."

"I said 'Lord I surrender to you,'" Gwen recalled. "I'm hearing voices from God and this is what God wants and I have to get this from God and if this is what God wants then I have to give it to him. So I went out and I bought a gun"

"The voices in her head told her it was time," Smith said. "And true to her value system, she had to obey. For her religion was not a therapeutic aid because of the way she had viewed it. Her God was a vengeful one, a violent one."

On Friday, August 17th, 1991 Gwen drove to Peterson Air Force Base to meet with her husband, a 75 mile drive, to bring him a change of clothes.

"Jim was working late and he asked me to bring him something to eat." Gwen said.

She had informed police that Jim was working all night to prepare for an inspection but changed his mind.

Gwen wrote in her journal about the incident.

When Jim called to say he was on his way home, I went into shock. I knew the time was at hand. I knew I wasn't really ready. I screamed and cried and raged. Then I asked again, if he was meant to die or was I just suckered into some kind of head game. Benjamin's daddy died. I cried myself to sleep that night. I thought what was I supposed to do with two husbands. God has the oddest sense of humor."

"She told me that she was gonna make a nice little picnic for them," Gwen's step-daughter Season recalled. "They were going to make a night of it and that she wanted him to feel good for his inspection."

Gwen left the home and dropped off both Season and son Ben with a friend. When Gwen arrived at the Air Force base, however, she stated that Jim told her that he was heading home. She maintained that the two then went back home in separate cars.

"His truck was in the lead," Gwen said. "I was in the car behind. I remember being so tired, I told him I can't go on anymore. I just want a quick nap and let's get in the back of the truck."

She said that they traveled in separate cars but she became tired and slept through the night at a rest stop along Interstate 25.

Police, however, believed that Gwen lured Jim to an abandoned stretch of highway with the promise of sex.

The two met at the side of the road and Gwen hesitated when thinking of pulling out the gun. She wanted her husband to go peacefully.

"I took the gun out from underneath the seat of the car," Gwen said. "I got into the truck and laid next to him and when I could feel that he was deeply sleeping that's when I shot him."

Gwen would shoot Jim six times.

"It was like I was outside of myself," Gwen said. "Looking and watching what I was doing. I felt very numb, very cold, like I was on auto-pilot. I got back into my car and I took apart the gun and I was just throwing the parts out the window and just driving around, just in a fog, not knowing what I was doing, where I was going. I stopped at a roadside rest stop. Fell asleep. When I woke up and I didn't know everything that happened."

When Gwen arrived back home that Saturday she began making calls to the police, stating that her husband was missing.

On Monday morning, she called Jim's supervisor who sent out two officers to search for him.

One of his co-workers would find his pickup truck on the side of Highway 83 in Douglas County. His body had been placed in the camper shell in back of his truck.

He had been shot six times in the chest and neck with a small caliber handgun.

Gwen would become the primary suspect.

Police noted that she hardly showed any emotion when they informed her of her husband's death.

"Her state of mind was that of a wife with a missing husband," one of the deputies recalled. "When she was telling a story, she couldn't stick with the same story. And that's a clue, obviously, to law enforcement."

Gwen would then break the news to Jim's daughter, Season.

"Gwen said they found him by the side of the road in his car," Season said. "And that he had been murdered. I don't remember her crying. It was the worst moment of my life."

Terry Knaack would be helpful in the case against Gwen. She had been secretly in love with him and given him her diary. He read through her writings and promptly delivered the diary to the Douglas County Sheriff's Department. The sheriffs then instructed him to call Gwen while they would listen in.

Gwen would tell Knaack that she didn't kill Jim but that she wanted to die. Then Douglas County Sheriff's Department Kim Castellano's intuition told her something was wrong. The Hendricks had two pre-teens, a boy and a girl and the boy was never around during questioning.

Castellano believed that Gwen had a problem with males. With one of the male investigators, an Air Force official, by her side, Castellano went back to talk to Gwen.

Once again, the boy was not there. Gwen was overly polite to Castellano, asking her if she wanted anything to eat and jumping up to fix her something before she could answer.

Gwen would totally ignored the male detective.

Castellano used this knowledge to her advantage and befriended Gwen, sensing that the delusional woman would be much more forthcoming with a female officer than a male.

Gwen began trusting her enough that she asked for Castellano's help in balancing her check book. The detective then saw that Hendricks had recently taken out several insurance policies that would be hers when her husband died.

The investigators then used a technique police refer to as the "midnight confession." Castellano and the Air Force official went over to the Hendricks house at eleven at night, waking Gwen up.

Questioning her in the family room, Gwen continued to deny her involvement in her husband's killing. Castellano and her partner then took turns reading from Gwen's journal, tightening the screws on her denial. They also saw Jim's watch on the counter.

Castellano then told her to get dressed and that she was being taken in.

Gwen finally cracked. She curled into a fetal position and confessed.

"Two stories that night—the story of the rest area and the story of Highway 83," she sobbed.

Gwen would go on to describe the highway story.

"There is blood everywhere, I can see it everywhere," she said. "It's terrible. My mind won't let me remember. I don't know if I shot him or not. I don't know what's real anymore."

Gwen was then taken to a local hospital where she stayed for two days for a mental health evaluation. She was arrested upon release and charged with her husband's murder.

After undergoing another mental health examination, Gwen was deemed delusional but understood the charges being levied against her.

Because of this, she was found fit to stand trial.

In court, however, Gwen continued to state that she didn't kill her husband. She said that the body found at the crime scene was not Jim's.

"There was the obvious choice for her attorneys to declare her insane," Smith said. "She had one hell of an imagination and could make things up on the fly. She said during the trial that she became completely convinced that her husband was still alive, going into full blown denial. 'He's still alive, he's out there somewhere and you have to find him', she would say. She was completely delusional."

Her first attorney, Lloyd Boyer, stated that it was physically impossible for Gwen to have murdered Jim Hendricks.

"The lack of gunshot residue inside the Capitol (Jim's car) vehicle," Boyer said. "Indicated that the murder had not occurred in the vehicle. Mr. Hendricks was quite a bit larger than Gwen and she was small, not especially strong and could not have moved the victim into the vehicle."

The investigators failed to produce the gun that Gwen used but the prosecution had another tool at its disposal.

The first link was Jim's watch that they found in Gwen's possession, which showed that she had tampered with the crime scene. The prosecution showed how she was going to use the money from the insurance policies and start a "home for troubled people" that would be near the spot where she killed her husband.

The jury found her guilty of first-degree murder and Hendricks was sentenced to life in prison.

"I just kept my faith that Jim would come rescue me and I would be set free from prison," Gwen said. "Of course, that never happened."

Inside the prison, physicians deemed her to be mentally unfit to be included with the general population and transferred her to the psychiatric unit.

"They got me on anti-psychotics," Gwen said. "And anti-depressants but it wasn't until 1997 that I started having memories of what had happened. At first, it was like just pictures and they hit me like bricks, you know. I killed a great husband and Dad. I robbed Season and Ben of their father. I felt lower than dirt."

She did have help, however, as some legal advocates filed briefs on her behalf, claiming that she had been insane at the time of her trial.

In September of 2000, the Supreme Court of Colorado overturned Gwen's conviction and ordered a new trial.

In April of 2001, a judge ruled that Gwen was not guilty by reason of insanity.

The trial lasted ten minutes.

"She came to terms with what she had done," Smith said. "She had stopped protesting, stop denying and admitted to what she had done."

Gwen was then remanded to a psychiatric care facility in Colorado. She then decided to change her name to "Emi Masai".

"When I lost Jim," Gwen said. "I also lost my children. I longed to be a wife and mother again. I redefined myself as married to Christ and being a mother to all the people I meet."

"By renaming herself she thought that she could obtain a new identity," Smith said. "It was a way of divorcing herself from her past transgressions."

Gwen went through four years of psychiatric treatment where the physicians determined that she was no longer a threat to society. She was released to a residential program where she now helps the needy at Mercy Ministries.

She continues to take her anti-psychotic medication.

"I never want to slip back into mental illness again," Gwen said. "I literally thank God every morning I open my medicine cabinet. I've always said justice wasn't done. Justice in this case would have been my execution. A life for a life. But it's not about fairness. It's about recognizing mental illness and knowing that you're not responsible for what you are doing when you're psychotic."

Gwen has had minimal contact with both her son and step-daughter since she committed the murder of their father.

"I long to see them but they let it be known through family channels that they don't want to see me," Gwen said. "So I respect that."

"I'm really glad that Gwen has helped herself enough to admit what she's done," Season said. "And I hope there never is a time where it gets easy for her to look in the mirror. Because there's never a time where it's easy to be without our Dad."

"I wish I could take it back," Gwen said. "Be a good wife and Mom again. I can't turn the clock back. So all I can do is give them my deepest apology and ask them to forgive me."